FAMILY AND SCHOOL

Book title: Family and School

© Maria Sideris

Copyright © 2016 by Anthi Sideris

Written by: A. Sideris, A. Brass, E. Glymitsa,
H. Tsirgioti, K. Economou

Translated by: Terry MacCallum

Edited by: Anatolie Fitopoulou

Production supervisor: www.mediterrabooks.com

Cover: Anthi Sideris

Publisher: Maria Sideris

ISBN: 978-618-82684-0-1

WRITTEN BY A GROUP OF EXPERTS

A. Sideris, A. Brass, E. Glymitsa, H. Tsirgioti, K. Economou

Family and School

AS

A Few Words

Persistence, patience and even more
persistence ... are some of
the virtues of parents
who light up the way
of their children's life.

They are the parents
who do not hold back
on the time and the love
they give their children...
Their light continues to shine
even in the next generations...

A few pages cannot
contain
the wealth of sentiments
that the existence of children
adds to our life,
nor can their happiness
be contained
in these few lines for
the heroes of their life...
us.

A.Sideri

*Dedicated
to my children,
Maria and Yannis,
and to the children
of the world*

Table of Contents

Acknowledgements   15

Introduction   17

CHAPTER 1

The Family: The Basis of Growth
and Personality Development in Children   21

   Our Place in the Family –
   The Creation of a Positive Environment   27

   The Family Constellation   29

   Our Expectations   32

   Family Meetings   34

   Pocket Money –
   Teaching Our Children How to Manage Money   38

   Moral Development   40

   Quarrelling and Fighting among Siblings –
   The Role of Parents   43

   Boys and Girls   46

   Sex Education   46

   Child Abuse – Child Neglect   48

   Loss of Loved Ones   50

   Multiple Roles and Conflicts   51

   Ensuring Free Time for Our Children   52

   The Internet   54

   The Broken Family   56

   Single-Parent Families   58

CHAPTER 2

Education: Preparing the Ground   61

   How to Become Better Parents   61

   Cultivating Our Emotional Intelligence   62

   Remaining True to Our Goals   67

Maintaining a Good Relationship with Our Child   68

Communicating Substantially with Our Child   68

Being Reliable and Consistent   69

Accepting Our Child Unconditionally   70

Being Careful Parents   70

Learning from Our Mistakes   71

Loving Our Children Unconditionally   72

Rewarding Our Child's Efforts and Accomplishments   73

How to Encourage our Child   75

How to Inspire   77

Setting Rules and Limits   78

Defining our Non-negotiable Principles   83

Violation of Rules and Limits:
Punishment - Reward - Explanation   84

Spending Quality Time with Our Child   87

Respecting Our Child   88

Love Is the Foundation Stone   88

CHAPTER 3

Kindergarten   91

How We as Parents Help Our Children Enter the First School of Life:
Kindergarten   93

What Does Kindergarten Offer Your Child?   95

How Is That Done? *Through Play*   97

Different Types of Play   98

Parents, Children and Play   100

Cooperation between the Kindergarten and the Family   102

Parental Participation in the Hygiene
of Kindergarten Pupils   104

How Parents Contribute to the Smooth Transition
of the Child into Primary School   104

CHAPTER 4

Primary School Begins   107

First Impressions   107

The New Primary School Pupil   111

First Contact between Parents and School   112

Cooperation, the Magic Word   112

How to Convey Positive Messages about the Importance
of School to Our Children   114

What Is Learning and How Is it Done?   116

Why Does a Child Learn?   117

What Makes Learning Difficult?   118

Combining Obligations and Needs   120

A Pupil's Job Is Tough...   121

Organising Study Time at Home   121

When and Under What Conditions
Should Study Take Place?   126

How Can we Facilitate Study Time for the Child?   130

How Can We Tell If Our Child Is Creatively Gifted?   133

The Development of Memory   136

Grading and Assessment in Primary School   139

Parent-Teacher Relationships   142

CHAPTER 5

The Psychosocial Development
of Preschool and School-Age Children   143

Childhood Friendships – Peer Groups   146

What Is the Most Appropriate Behaviour
on the Part of Parents?   147

CHAPTER 6

Summer Holidays   149

CHAPTER 7

Transition from Primary to Secondary School   153

Factors Affecting the Transition   154

Parental Attitudes.   155

CHAPTER 8

School Adjustment Difficulties 157

When Is Problematic Behaviour Considered Serious? 159

Psychological and Conduct Disorders 161

  A. Disorders of Psychological Development 161

    a. Specific developmental disorders
of speech and language 162

    b. Specific speech articulation disorder 162

    1. *Phonological disorder* 163

    2. *Stuttering* 163

    c. Expressive language disorder 164

    d. Receptive language disorder 164

  B. Learning Difficulties - Specific Developmental
Disorders of Scholastic Skills 164

    a. Specific reading disorder (developmental dyslexia) 167

    b. Specific spelling disorder 167

    c. Disorder of written expression
(dysorthographia, dysgraphia) 167

    d. Specific disorder of arithmetical skills (dyscalculia) 168

    e. Mixed disorder of scholastic skills 169

The Role of the Family in Dealing with Children
with Learning Difficulties 169

  C. Disorders of Behaviour and Emotion 172

    a. Attention Deficit - Hyperactivity Disorder (ADHD) 172

Diagnosis of ADHD 173

Causes of ADHD 174

  1. Genetic 174

  2. Brain growth and function 175

  3. Family - Social - Environmental 176

Treating ADHD 176

What Parents Should Do 177

b. Aggressive Behaviour   179

Family Factors   183

Environmental Factors   184

Television Viewing   184

Peers   185

Training Parents on How to Deal
with Aggressive Behaviour   185

Victimisation-Bullying (The Other Perspective)   186

c. School refusal – Anxiety   188

d. Childhood Timidity, Shyness, Introversion,
and Loneliness   193

What factors Contribute to the Maintenance
of Timidity in Children?   194

What Should Parents Do?   195

Experiences and the Unconscious   197

Epilogue   199

Author Resumes   200

Reviews - Comments from parents
and educators   205

REFERENCES   211

Greek Bibliography   211

Foreign Bibliography   215

Acknowledgements

IT IS VERY IMPORTANT for someone to have great colleagues who all share a common vision and wish to create something great, something that will remain in the mind and the heart of parents who want to make a difference as far as raising their children is concerned; in short, those parents who regard what they do a *calling* and not a job.

I would like to thank family counsellor, Anastasios Brass, who with his vast experience, the experience of many years, and the deep knowledge of how a family functions, has outdone himself in presenting all aspects of family life and highlighting the most suitable environment in which parents can raise their children to become decent adults.

I'd also like to thank Eleni Tsirgioti, Headmistress Preschool Education, for her eagerness and contribution to this study of great importance, which focuses on the development of children during their preschool years when they develop physically, emotionally, intellectually and socially and become prepared for the next educational steps, which are primary and secondary school.

I also give thanks to the teacher, Efi Glimitsa, for the passion that distinguishes her teaching methods, her ingenuity, her well-placed examples and her suggestions concerning techniques and strategies parents can use to support their children in their effort to deal with the demands of primary school.

I thank Katerina Economou, a psychologist for children, adolescents and adults, for her precious and priceless observations in the chapter "Experiences and the Unconscious".

I would also like to thank my parents and siblings, who always encouraged me and supported me in my choices.

I thank you all from the bottom of my heart.

Introduction

THE BOOK YOU ARE HOLDING IN YOUR HANDS was mainly written because of our intense desire to convey what we consider essential knowledge as well as the most effective ways for parents to fulfil their role and achieve their goal: to raise decent adults. With the love and passion we have for children as our guide, we gathered theories and practices, experiences of parents, observations of family counsellors, psycho-educational analyses by scientists and teachers. Our aim was to provide the tools to make the transition of children from kindergarten to primary school as smooth as possible, to ensure their healthy adjustment to the family and school environment and to support them on their "journey" on the ship of knowledge and socialisation that will not only prepare them for their greater journey of academic achievement but also assist them along the path toward self-actualisation.

We all have the experience of being a parent. However, our mission – raising children – is the only scientific subject that is not taught in any university. It is ironic that, while the role of a parent constitutes one of the most important values of life, we are called upon to perform this play without an audition or rehearsals. And so, we have no choice but to play this role as best we can for the sake of our children and our own sake.

The education of a child is of primary importance. It nurtures and shapes the completed and balanced personality of a person who knows how to appreciate the beauty of life and enjoy the pleasure of creating and giving. It is, however, a joint effort. The parents, on the one hand, and the state through its educational institutions, on the other, play an equally important and complementary role in achieving their common objectives. In the family, the children live within a framework set by the parents. The contribution of the family plays a decisive role in the development of young people's character and personality, especially at a young age.

The aim of this book is to inform parents about this difficult task because the better-informed parent is better equipped to appreciate the issues related to the learning environment of children and their cognitive and psychosocial development. Thus, by understanding where to focus their attention; that is, by comprehending the reasons for their child's behaviour, they can better cooperate and communicate with the teachers, who are their most important allies in the difficult task of raising children.

In the first years of our children's lives, we have many questions and concerns about whether we will be able to meet all their biological needs: food, sleep and hygiene, so that they will want for nothing and be cheerful and happy. With the passing of time, as our child grows, we face situations and problems that make us feel that our reservoirs of love may not be enough. This feeling creates concerns and insecurities and leads us to make erroneous judgments and to act impulsively and then fall into the vicious circle of doubts and guilt.

This book shows how parents, through their own maturity and reassessment in relation with the development of their child, can become more able to talk with their child, to comprehend their child, to channel their love more effectively and creatively and to support, inspire and encourage it in its endeavours.

On reading this book, you will see that we start by extensively analysing the institution of family and the role it plays in the shaping of a child's healthy personality.

Then, we present a detailed analysis on what methods to follow in order to apply desirable parental behaviour. This is done for two main reasons:

a. Because for all problematic behaviour that arises along the way, experts go back to the family in order to pinpoint areas where parents erred in the upbringing of their children. In this book, you will find an analysis of the factors that contribute to the fertile and effective education of your children.

b. In order to facilitate the child's entry into the new reality – school – and to all the future schools it will attend in its life. It is easier for the child to acquire these foundations when it is still young. The core of a person's personality is shaped during the first five years of life. During these five very important years, the child discovers the reality that surrounds him, observes the world around him and forms attitudes and beliefs.

The effort we make to raise our children properly is a life investment. We see the results of our labours on a daily basis in our children when these efforts are sincere, organised and systematic. It is the effort we make to play our role as best we can with the final goal of preparing our children to face the difficulties of childhood, adolescence and later, adult life.

Enjoy the book!

CHAPTER 1

The Family: The Basis of Growth and Personality Development in Children

A VERY IMPORTANT ASPECT OF OUR LIFE is that of companionship. It is our decision to choose a companion and to begin our journey on a new path. The path of family life.

What is paradoxical is that during all our years of school life and later during our university studies, no one spoke to us or taught us how to live lovingly and harmoniously with the companion of our choice. Even our family did not speak to us in an organised and serious way about this matter. We only acquired scattered knowledge and experience, either positive or negative, along the way while living within our family. Thus, when that blessed hour arrives, it is very likely that we will not have formed the foundations on which we can stand in order to build our relationship and create a healthy family.

We know, of course, that the family is the smallest social unit that changes continuously and develops with the passage of time. Its members are connected, or rather should be connected, with emotional bonds of love, respect and appreciation that, if they last for years, make it strong and happy. Each member has their own role within this system: this role does not remain constant but varies according to age and with the changes in the social environment.

If we wish to have a successful marriage, it should occur after serious thought and it should be the product of a conscious decision. Though it is essential that we realise it requires continuous effort and great will.

If the couple share common goals and have taken the decision to fight for them, then they will experience genuine satisfaction. This will help them lay the foundations for a happy life, not only for themselves, but above all, for their children.

As we have pointed out already, no one spoke to us in a serious, organised and well-founded manner about subjects such as how to avoid the boredom of marriage; what to expect during pregnancy, childbirth and after birth and the role of the father; and, how to best raise our children. But let's take things one at a time, because all of the above affect the companionship of the couple, the healthy development of the marriage and, consequently, the shaping of the children's personality.

$$\maltese \qquad \maltese$$

The couple gets married and the honeymoon period is spent exchanging hugs and kisses. One is interested in and takes care of the other. The newly-weds talk to each other and find solutions to their problems with understanding, without bias or ulterior motives.

Little by little, however, with the passage of time, the hugs and discussions decrease. Gradually, the number of disagreements increase, soon after the conflicts emerge, the relationship grows lax and soon grows cold.

If during this period the couple has acquired children, then everything that happens in the couple affects the children and inevitably influences their character and behaviour (insecurities, phobias, aggressiveness, etc.).

Of course, it is natural for a couple to have disagreements. These disagreements, however, should not reach the point of conflict, especially in front of the children, who often feel responsible, and thus, apart from other things, also feel guilt. Problems are not solved with conflict and shouting. On the contrary, they usually become greater because words said in anger usually hurt and increase tension. If conflict and shouting don't solve the problem, why do couples treat each other, as well as their children, in this way?

Because they were born and grew up in an environment where disagreements were usually resolved in this way. What should be done? This behaviour pattern should change. Is it easy to do so? Not always. It is however possible, especially if we and our children really want to live peacefully.

❦   ❦

What should we do in order to achieve this peacefulness? Not allow boredom to enter our marriage. How can we do this? By trying to renew our relationship in various ways, with surprises and changes in our behaviour towards each other. For example, we can greet our companion with a hot embrace when he/she returns home. A sweet message sent on the mobile, a written message on the bathroom mirror, a message of love in a note that will be discreetly placed in our companion's pocket. A walk that had not been planned, a gift that will be given in an original way, a flower offered with a lot of love.

If our imagination is given free rein and there is a genuine desire for change, many inexpensive ways will be found to keep boredom at bay forever. In fact, the marriage will blossom and will fill our souls with beautiful and pleasant sentiments. In this case, our own joy, satisfaction and happiness will also be conveyed to our children, with all the positive consequences.

We should not, however, leave the following question unanswered: what should we do to ease the repercussions in the relationship between the parents and their children when disagreement turns into tension and then into conflict? The first thing we should do is consider whether the intensity and the conflict resolve the problem or exacerbate it. And, naturally, because the conclusion we will reach is that not only does it not solve the problem, but in fact, makes it bigger, we should find a way to minimise the disagreement when it escalates in intensity.

The first step is for everyone to calm down and sit side by side and discuss the problem using key words that ease the tension (e.g. *what* is to blame and not *who* is to blame). Is it easy to stop what has begun? Yes, it is, if we want our own and our children's peace of mind. Experts have recommended many techniques, which we sometimes use, though not systematically. One way is to tell our companion that we do not wish to quarrel. If despite this they continue, then we could withdraw into another room or, even more effectively, we can say: "I'm going for a walk to calm down, and to give you the chance to calm down as well, and when I return, and if you want to, we can discuss it."

We've already mentioned that young people are not informed about pregnancy, childbirth and post birth. Women receive some kind of briefing from other women but men are usually left completely in the dark.

Let's take things one at a time. A woman gets pregnant. The man observes the changes and, to a certain extent, understands his companion. He sees her belly growing, sees her becoming heavier, sees her breathing with greater difficulty and is willing to fulfil any of her wishes and respond to her needs.

However, at the back of his mind he believes that after the baby is born he will again find the woman he has married. After the baby is born, the man quickly realises that he has a new woman before him, one with different problems and behaviours. He was not expecting this because no one had informed him.

As a result, he may misinterpret his wife's behaviour. He may start to believe that she is only interested in her child and has him on the margin. He shapes his own behaviour according to these beliefs and,

instead of supporting his wife in her attempt to overcome the psychosomatic changes occurring to her, he becomes distant and displays
negative behaviours. If there is no one at this phase to help him understand what's going on with his wife, the marriage can reach the
point of divorce.

There is no doubt that it is very important for the couple to attend
to their own relationship, and not only to their role as parents, so that
they can also develop as companions.

It is a period of intense stress and anxiety and just as things begin
to fall into place, there is often the arrival of a second child. The couple is more experienced now and everything flows more smoothly. On
the other hand, though, the relationship between the couple becomes
more complicated because the siblings now start to develop their own
relationship. Moreover, more problems may emerge because of jealousy between the children.

Did the parents prepare their first child for the arrival of its younger
sibling? Were they careful about how they behaved from the moment
the mother left in order to go give birth until she returned home with
the new baby? When the mother is nursing or attending to the baby,
is somebody occupied with the older child or does the mother involve
it in the baby's care?

When relatives and friends come to see the new baby, they will
ease the feelings of jealousy the older child may exhibit if they initially
spend time with it before turning to the newborn. Most likely, the child
will display normal levels of jealousy, which should not have any serious negative repercussions or cause problems for the parents.

If there is a relationship of love between the parents and they make
sure that all members of the family feel that they are equal, then such
situations will be avoided.

The parents will also face difficulties when they decide to send their child to nursery school. When it concerns an only child, things are simpler. The parents have plenty of time to prepare the child and when it goes to nursery school, it may have many or few difficulties adjusting. Together with the proper guidance of experts at the nursery school, everything will fall into place. However, when there are also other children, especially younger ones, there are usually more serious issues and problems that are more complicated.

The child who has to go to nursery school often feels that he is being removed from the home and the family and feelings of jealousy and abandonment often appear, accompanied by the corresponding reactions. For this reason, the parents should speak with the child and show him that their love and their interest will remain the same. They should explain that they are sending it to nursery school so that it will have a better time, so that it can acquire friends and play. When it returns home though, it should be met with a warm reception and some quality time with a parent.

The entry of children into nursery school, and later kindergarten, allows parents to have more time for themselves. This is particularly important for the mother because it allows her to work and develop her career and thus offer more to her family. The father continues to work but now also participates in the upbringing of the children.

Parents should not feel guilty for sending their child to nursery school: this separation is beneficial for the child, especially when it is two years old and older. Usually, when a mother is continuously with her child, "it is smothered" and becomes spoiled. On the other hand, children become more independent and sociable when they participate in other social groups, such as those in a nursery school and later kindergarten.

OUR PLACE IN THE FAMILY -
THE CREATION OF A POSITIVE ENVIRONMENT

The couple has acquired one or more children. What they now desire is to provide their children with a proper upbringing. They will succeed in doing so, provided that they try to understand their child, since the emotions and the behaviour of children are quite different from those of adults.

Parents are bound to their children since they are the ones that brought them into the world and have undertaken to raise them. They are the ones solely responsible for the family they have created. How will they raise them however? What type of environment is best suited to provide them with everything they will need to face the remainder of their life? Of course, it is the environment in which parental values and models of correct behaviour are cultivated by the parents themselves and are "passed on" to the children in a natural way and without laborious efforts.

Child psychiatrist Dimitris Karagiannis points out that children live within the framework laid down by the parents. On a conscious level, parents want what's best for their children. It is obvious, however, that only they have the ability and the strength to change things. In other words, they shape the family context. Therefore, we need to observe how parents define the family atmosphere and how they shape certain situations of family life to the extent that they may cause psychological trauma, which may accompany the child to adulthood.

❀   ❀

If there is mutual respect and esteem between the father and the mother, the children perceive that these are the most common and familiar models of behaviour they should cultivate in their own relationships with other people other than family members. When the father and the mother have a relationship based on understanding and emotional communication, on helping and supporting the other, on encouragement, trust, room for personal development; if, in other words, a positive family atmosphere is created and maintained, then the children are given the opportunity to live authentic experiences, and have their parents as role models in relationships. What can be more beautiful for children than to see 'love in action' in the relationship of the two most significant people in their life?

Of course, there is always the likelihood that differing opinions will be expressed and conflicts between the couple may arise, but the greatest lessons parents can offer their children is how to resolve these conflicts. All people are different from each other and that's why there are different attitudes towards life. When, however, the conflict is resolved with real interest and understanding, when the negative atmosphere and the tension disappear with a hug, the children feel secure. In this way, they gradually shape their character.

Actually, at what age does a child's character start to take shape and how long does it last? A person's character is shaped from in utero until around the age of 20. During pregnancy, the mother not only gives food to the foetus but also transmits emotions. If one has a calm pregnancy, then, usually a calm baby is born. If one has a pregnancy filled with tension, conflict, sorrow, serious family problems, then a restless baby will be born. The child's character has already begun to take shape.

Then follows the period of the first five years of a child's life. During these five years, the most serious foundations of a child's character are formed. A child is born with all the positive and negative characteristics an individual can have. Which ones it will keep and which ones it will discard depends on the environment in which it will live. We must not forget that up until the age of five it will acquire millions of experiences, some of which it will keep while others it will reject because the child will have nothing to gain from them.

Therefore, by the age of five the child has shaped a large part of its character and, to a great degree, its personality. In the beginning, a child is pressed by its biological needs (for sleep, food, play) and wants them satisfied. Later, it develops its memory and is aware of its bodily state. Thus it begins to perceive its surrounding reality. The environment – in the beginning the family, later the nursery school, kindergarten, school and, finally, the broader social environment – plays a big and important role in the shaping of its character.

The child will therefore develop well if these factors help him. It will repeat whatever gives it the feeling that it has found its place and will abandon whatever makes it feel out of place.

THE FAMILY CONSTELLATION

It is very useful and helpful to be able to interpret the reactions of children in the same family and particularly depending on the order in which they have been born. The family constellation refers to the psychological position each child holds in the family in relation to his/her siblings.

The first child is an only child for a certain time period, up until the arrival of the second child. The second child and the all others that follow will always have to deal with somebody who precedes them – unless the older sibling is mentally or physically disabled. The first child loses his uniqueness and henceforth has to share everything with someone else who usually demands their share and their place in the family quite dynamically. As a result, the until-recently only child displays symptoms of jealousy. Parents should prepare their child for the arrival of a sibling from the pregnancy. Most important, however, is that they behave correctly after the birth of the sibling in order that the jealousy is limited to within normal contexts.

Each child struggles for a place in the family in any way it feels greater certainty that it will achieve it. For example, if Maria, who is the first child, is very good at theoretical school subjects, Yannis, who is the second child, will try to distinguish himself in the practical subjects in order to find his place in the family – a place equally as worthy as Maria's. Usually siblings with a smaller age difference are more competitive. Irrespective of family size, greater competition usually exists between the first and the second child. These two, at least for a certain time period, are the only children that have to define their place in the family.

If a third child enters the family, the second child becomes the middle child and things become even more complicated. While up to this point the second child has been trying to assert his place in the family, he suddenly finds himself between clashing rocks. He feels under pressure, deprived of the privileges enjoyed by the first and third child. Thus we say that it goes through the 'middle child syndrome".

The third and youngest child learns to take advantage of the fact that it is the baby of the family. Perhaps it seeks its place by being cute or clumsy, cooperative or reactive, compliant or domineering – in any case, it seeks the constant attention of parents who fall into the trap.

In general, children are quite successful at getting parents to fall into the traps they set them. We should not forget that children are, unfortunately, more patient and persistent than parents.

However, let's also talk about the only child and twins.

The only child shapes its character, its personality and its behaviour by living in a monopolistic system. Everything is only the child's: the parents, the relatives, the house, the toys, the interest, the love. It has not learned to share and for this reason it comes into conflict with other children when it happens to find itself among them. It lays down the rules of the game and is the only one that has the right to make demands. This often puts its parents in a difficult position and the only child itself often becomes isolated and shuts itself off. The fact that it mainly lives with adults shapes a particular type of personality and often leads to behaviour with bizarre mood swings. The child may be talkative and cheerful one moment, and silent and aggressive the next; or it may appear to be spoiled. And there is always the possibility that it may mature too quickly or forever remain a baby.

Are all only children like that? Of course not. The character and behaviour they display will depend on the closer or broader family environment.

Will the environment be overprotective and ready to satisfy every wish of the child without limits and rules or will it help it grow normally, meaning, without excessive requirements, but willing to take what corresponds to him? It should learn to share what it has with others, whether that is material goods or sentiments. It should not escape our notice that very often children ask their parents for a sibling, the lack of which they may never overcome during their lifetime.

Now, let's take a look at twins. Twins hold an interesting place in the family constellation. Quite a few parents tend to dress them alike and to treat them as if they are one and the same. Parents do not deal with them as separate individuals and in so doing, do not help them each grow up and shape their own character and personality. When this happens, there are two possible outcomes: either each child struggles to acquire a perfectly separate identity or tries to take the place of the first or second child, since they are well aware who was born first and who second.

The role the parents play during this process, whereby the children secure a place in the family and in society, is important and decisive because, depending on the way they face their children, they either encourage or discourage them, thus contributing to the shaping of their character and influencing their development in either a positive or negative way.

Certain parents, in their own way, without necessarily meaning to, encourage this sibling rivalry either by praising the virtues of the child that better represents their values or by ignoring or judging the other child. If parents realise what's going on and stop criticising the one child while continuously praising the other, then the different child can become more collaborative and begin to distinguish itself in other sectors.

Moreover, we should point out that the children in a family are competitive with each other but this can be turned into a healthy form of competition that is creative and may have positive results. It depends on how tactfully the parents handle the situation.

On the other hand, we should never forget that if parents accept their child unconditionally, then the children will not feel the need to claim their place in the family. Even less so when we stress, in all sincerity, how unique our child is and recognise the daily challenges it has to face, some of which it will conquer – while others will defeat him: "You are my unique and beloved daughter! You are my unique and beloved son!"

Our Expectations

Usually, either consciously or unconsciously, parents "pass on" their unfulfilled dreams to the future of their child. All our unfulfilled dreams become the expectations we have of our child. We expect our children to become something other than what is within the scope of their abilities in order to achieve what we did not achieve in our life. We often accompany these expectations with the common phrase: "in order to succeed in life..."

How would we like our child to be when it enters the arena of life?

A successful professional who is cheerful and gets satisfaction from his daily work or a miserable, unsatisfied person who has no appetite for the work he does?

We believe that you will all agree with the one and only answer. That's why we as parents should not block the genuine and innate tendency of children to reveal their real talents. What's more, what we can do, since we are more mature and can see things more holistically and from a distance, is try to help them discover these talents, and once they've discovered them, to help them make good use of them in making their choices: those that will offer satisfaction and happiness.

If, on the other hand, we do not rid ourselves of our binding behaviour, we should realise that in this way we are condemning our children to follow professions that they may one day discover do not suit them. We have enough examples of children who did what their parents wanted. They sacrificed a few years of their life on studies they had no interest in and after receiving their degree they followed the profession they themselves desired.

Our children are not an extension of ourselves, as we so often hear, but an extension of life. We are supposed to encourage and support them so that they may move forward. They alone will set their objectives and find their way as they grow up. They may wander until they find what's best for them but in the end they will find it and it will suit them. The only thing we have to do is give them love and support.

We must bear in mind that the needs of people change with the times and just like we moved forward from where our own parents left off in order to respond to the needs of the present society, so will our own children be called upon to face the future demands of society.

Our role is to give children the space they need in order to develop, to get to know themselves, to make dreams and to take their decisions. What we can do – after we have laid the foundations for our children from a young age – is accompany them and offer our opinion. In this way, children will acquire the strength to assert themselves, to achieve their goals and, at the same time, to protect themselves.

FAMILY MEETINGS

It is the so-called "family council", which can become quite dynamic and contribute positively to the growth of cooperation and mutual respect between family members.

The family meeting is a scheduled gathering of family members, during which plans are drawn up, various activities are scheduled, decisions on various subjects are taken, problems are solved, and in general, there is discussion about whatever the parents feel should be shared with the children in order that decisions be taken jointly and democratically.

An essential prerequisite is that these meetings should not take place in order to solve problems because interest will quickly decline and family members will be looking for excuses to be absent, which in essence will mean the cancellation of this family institution.

Steps should, however, be taken to prevent this from happening because family meetings give family members the opportunity to:

1. Be heard

2. Express positive feelings for other family members

3. Give encouragement

4. Contribute so that various household chores are fairly shared

5. Express their thoughts, ideas, feelings as well as their complaints

6. Help resolve differences and face recurring problems

7. Participate in the planning of family entertainment

In order for these meetings to be effective, they should be held once a week or fortnight on a regular basis. You should choose the most suitable time when the family can come together more easily.

The parents are the coordinators of the meetings until the children reach school age. As the children grow and enter puberty, they too can take on the role of coordinator. As soon as young children can communicate, they may participate in the family meetings. They may get tired and wish to leave earlier. It does not matter; you should continue encouraging your children to take part.

In each meeting, you should try to:

a. give all members the opportunity to present their ideas. It is preferable, at least during the first meetings, to allow the children to speak first. Afterwards, the parents can add other ideas. This is important because, otherwise, the children may feel that the meetings are held in order for the parents to impose their ideas. "Who has something to say? Mary, you haven't said anything. Do you have anything to suggest?"

b. encourage everybody to present topics for discussion. If a long time period intervenes between two meetings, members should be encouraged to jot down topics for discussion the moment they arise so that they are not forgotten by the time the next meeting occurs. In this way, everybody learns to be organised.

c. prevent complaints and arguments from occurring during the meeting. Instead, ask family members for ideas on how to solve the problem. Ask if anybody can suggest a solution.

d. plan family entertainment. Each week, plan entertainment or a shared activity for the entire family. You can go on an outing, see a film, go to the theatre, take a walk in the city centre, etc. If this activity requires some preparation, jointly decide who should do what and have members commit to the task they have been appointed to do.

Of course, we should bear in mind that if adolescents are involved, they might not always be willing to participate in these shared activities. Parents should be lenient towards their desire to differentiate themselves; they should discuss it with them and not insist on their participation.

e. open numerous other topics for discussion and decision-making: e.g. the menu, family finances and budgeting, pocket money, conflicts between siblings, the planning of free time, entertainment activities for the whole family, etc.

Family finances and pocket money are subjects that should preoccupy us more deeply. It is good for children to have a general picture of their family's financial situation. If they don't, they may make excessive demands, such as expensive clothes, more pocket money, costly excursions, etc. As a result, complaints, reactions and conflicts that cause bitterness and upheaval to the family life ensue. If, on the other hand, the children are aware of the family's financial situation, not only do they accept the restrictions on expenses, but they are also willing to help so that there is some financial balance and peace in the family regarding this matter.

f. make decisions with everybody's consent; that is to say, try to reach a general consensus. There will be times, however, when not everyone will agree. If you reach a dead end, ask for ideas again. If after numerous attempts the family still fails to reach a joint decision, then the parents will have to take the decision alone. You can, however, decide to set the issue aside temporarily, giving family members a little extra time to think things through, and re-discuss the matter at the next meeting. Be careful! Explain the reason for the temporary deferral and never take any decision in anger or in vengeance because then you will face resistance. If there is little time to spare, then try to arrange a new meeting and discussion so that the children may take part in the decision-making.

During family meetings, parents should have patience, remain calm and encourage members to participate, make suggestions and reach joint decisions so as to avoid having negative reactions when the time comes to apply the decisions.

g. restate the decisions that have been taken and ask members to commit to them.

h. share pleasant feelings about happy events that took place during the week. A word of praise for academic performance, a reward for good behaviour or good budgeting, the results of a pleasant activity, etc.

If you cannot assemble all the family members, either because they do not want to devote their time or because they generally disagree with the idea, then have the meeting with the members that agree. The others may decide to participate later, after they see the benefits of taking part.

Even though family meetings are not a panacea for all family problems, they are especially beneficial for children. They learn to participate in problem solving, they acquire self-confidence when they see that we ask for their opinion in solving problems and listen to them carefully, they become committed to carrying out decisions, all of which cultivate their sense of responsibility. In a nutshell, we are given the chance to treat them as equals, and in so doing, teach them to respect others through our example. In this way, they learn to function as a team and that is how they will handle problems in the future as adults wherever they may find themselves.

The essence of this family habit is to help family members adopt a cooperative, democratic method with which they will learn to handle the common matters that occupy them. Perhaps these meetings are not held on a regular basis, but are called in an emergency when a specific event that needs discussion occurs. When your children ask for a meeting to be held in order to discuss something, then you know you have succeeded! (Dinkmeyer & McKay, 2007)

POCKET MONEY -
TEACHING OUR CHILDREN HOW TO MANAGE MONEY

Many parents face the dilemma regarding when and how much money they should give their children for their weekly expenses. This is especially true nowadays, during these times of financial crises, when the family income is greatly limited.

Pocket money is very important because children acquire a sense of responsibility and learn to manage the sum of money given to them by their parents. However, when we give children money, we must also teach them how to spend it wisely.

At what age we should begin giving a child money depends on the child's level of maturity. Between the ages of six and seven, children conceive that certain things are worth more than others. Between the ages of seven and eight, they understand the equivalence that exists between the price of an item and its value in currency. Between the ages of eight and nine, they have learned how to count and calculate and face no problem regarding the change.

It is therefore up to the parents to decide, after having assessed the needs of their child, the sum of money they will give their child on a regular basis, e.g. every 2-3 days. If the parents see that their children manage their money wisely, then they can give them the amount of money they have agreed on less frequent intervals, e.g. every Monday, all the while checking how the money is being managed.

❦ ❦

You should remain consistent on the agreed-upon sum even if your child has spent it faster than predicted, and a relevant discussion should take place. The next time, the child will be more careful and it will learn to make wiser purchases. The child must learn that not all its desires will be fulfilled and that the money you are willing to spend is not unlimited.

It is very important that money not be given as a reward for anything, e.g. good marks, good behaviour, etc., because in this way children are given the impression that everything has a price and that money can compensate for everything.

Also, children should not be deprived of their pocket money as a form of punishment, e.g. for not doing homework or for having damaged something, because in this way we convey the wrong message concerning the cause and the solution of a problem.

On the other hand, you should never give beyond your means simply because you suffered deprivation as a child. It is true that this will make you feel better but it doesn't help children learn to appreciate and manage their money.

Throughout this process, it is also very important that money not be given to children from others in their environment (e.g. from relatives, grandparents) because then children will lose track of how much money they can spend; a lesson you have diligently tried to teach them. As a result, children will never learn to manage their money.

Children must learn that it is their responsibility to budget their money. This is a lesson that will benefit them throughout their life.

Moral Development

With the term 'morality', we mean a system with which we evaluate a person's actions.

The basic aim of the socialisation process is to render the child capable of recognising what is moral and what is immoral, what is bad and what is good, what is correct and what is wrong in one's own behaviour and in the behaviour of others, with a view to making one's actions an expression of internalised rules of behaviour, so that one acts "correctly" even when there is no threat of punishment, e.g. one does not steal or trespass on another's property, one respects the value of human life, obeys the rules, keeps promises, etc.

Three are the elements that make up morality, and we will analyse them, mainly in relation to the role of parents:

   a. *Knowledge of moral rules.* We, the parents, should, depending on the child's age, teach it the moral rules according to which our society functions.

   b. *The emotional side of morality.* It is related with the type of emotions we feel when we do a good deed (internal satisfaction, jubilation) or an immoral act (guilt, shame).

   c. *One's main behaviour as action.* It is the element with the greatest gravity in the formation of morality.

Usually, the child understands which actions are not moral from the punishment imposed by the parents. A child commits a prohibited action, the parent imposes psychological punishment on the child and this punishment causes stress. When this is repeated enough times, the offense will be connected with the stress that it causes without the punishment necessarily intervening. In order to reduce the stress, the child suppresses the prohibited action.

Scientists recommend that parents should make the child feel stress not for the action itself but for the consequences that this action can have on others. We explain the consequences of the child's action on the emotions of others, e.g. "Don't make a mess because mum will get more tired cleaning it up" or "I get upset when I see you destroying your desk." If the child feels compassion for and a desire to please those around him – if, in other words, he has positive emotions – he will more easily adapt to this tactic and will be deterred from committing the action.

Parents can considerably influence the formation of morality in the child via its personality and behaviour as follows:

a. *The morality of the parent.* The most important factor in the moral growth of a child is its identification with the parent. The more developed and complete the morality of the parent is, the stronger the moral conscience and the feelings of guilt a child will have. In contrast, the weaker the morality of the parent, the looser and more ineffective the moral armoury of the child is. As for this, the type of relationship between the child and the parent is of primary importance. The closer and warmer this relationship is, the greater the identification with the parent. Difficulties in the identification process arise when the parent is absent (orphaned children, children of divorced parents who have no communication with one of the two parents, etc.).

b. The two parents have *consistent criteria* concerning what is permitted and what is not, and they should be *consistent* in their disciplinary practices. When parents apply disciplinary practices consistently, then the child feels safe. They must also define the limits within which the child can move around freely but should not surpass. These limits should be clearly defined and both parties should be aware of them.

When a child faces an unreliable parent, it cannot predict his/her reactions, and as a result, the child loses the sense that he can control his environment. Children with this perception of the world have difficulty developing what J.B. Rotter calls an "internal locus of control." These children end up believing that their fate is in the hands of others and they develop a passive attitude towards life.

c. *The use of rational analysis of the consequences of one's actions.* The most effective way of reinforcing moral behaviour is by analysing the consequences a child's action has on the emotions of others. Thus, the child is equipped with greater resistance toward the challenges that trigger problematic behaviour.

d. The imposed punishment should be *specific, consistent, immediate* and *proportional* to the offense. More specifically, it should address the act and not the child. It is the action that is punished and not the child. A child is accepted unconditionally, though its actions may at times be accepted while at others not. "I am punishing you because with this action you hurt your brother." We never impose a punishment when we are out of control, and we never use the phrases, "I don't love you" or "Go away, you're a bad child", which are completely non-pedagogical.

e. *Portraying moral models for imitation.* It is clear that a child has stronger motives to develop morality if he has a parent who behaves according to a set of moral values as a role model than if the parent is either inconsistent towards his principles or without the necessary morality one must be characterised by.

Therefore, in order for a child to acquire a strong sense of morality, the parent should be affectionate, maintain a warm relationship with the child and express a positive attitude towards one's fellowmen and environment. Parents should analyse and explain to the child the negative consequences its actions may have on the feelings of others and they should set the example by putting these reasonable and mature moral criteria into practice, as they require others to do. (Paraskevopoulos, 1985)

QUARRELLING AND FIGHTING AMONG SIBLINGS – THE ROLE OF PARENTS

Usually, when children fight, they do so to attract their parents' attention. Very soon, the parents take on the role of referee and become involved in the power struggle. They fall into the trap and intervene, usually shouting as well, and allocate justice, verbally or practically.

Parents should know that most of the times the children's quarrels are "set up". In other words, they take place in order to punish the "giant" parents or in order to see whose side the parents will take and reach a conclusion concerning who they love more. Thus, they have played their game and have thrown the parents into the trap.

Certain parents believe that they are acting fairly if they punish both sides equally. However, in this case, at least one child will feel he has been wronged. Whose problem is it? Certainly not the parents'. What can parents do? Remain indifferent and let the children argue until they tear down the house?

There are tactics that, if applied, can deal with the problem. In order to do so, you must be equipped with patience and persistence because the children usually have both of these characteristics and so come out the "winners".

If the children are young, you should try to draw their attention with something else, e.g. tell them that you're going out for an ice-cream or to the playground and that you're sorry that they will have to stay home and bicker (of course, the other parent or some other adult should be in the house). You must put your imagination to work in order to come up with similar tactics that will prove effective in dealing with your children. In the end, they usually rush to follow the parents and forget about their quarrel.

When the children are older, the parents should appear to be in-different, keeping a distance from the quarrel and, if possible, going into another room. With this tactic, the children lose all interest in the quarrel because they do not succeed in involving the parents. If the children insist that the parents take sides, then the latter should say in a serious and indifferent tone: "This concerns you, solve your problems alone and go play".

Because we are talking about slightly older children, parents should make sure that leaving them in the same room is absolutely safe.

If, however, the parents get involved in the argument, the message they are going to 'send' to their children is that a third party can solve their problems instead of solving them by themselves. Arguments are common but not normal. Children can learn to live without fighting. They will learn to avoid them as soon as they learn how to solve their own problems. Thus, we should not seek to take sides in their fights or arguments because they need to learn through the physical consequences of their actions (negative feelings, sadness, anger, grief).

Of course, if we are concerned that one of the two children might hurt themselves, we should break them up, even though most arguments between siblings do not result in injuries.

You may be wondering about what happens when one of the children is an innocent victim. Obviously, this does happen but how can we help that child to learn to protect itself if we continually step up to protect it?

You might say: All's well, but, what happens when the older children fight with the younger ones? In this case, we need to step in immediately. Of course, the younger children might try to take advantage of the fact by trying to make us protect them. If, for example, seven-year-old Maria and fourteen-year-old Peter go too far, we should quietly and respectfully tell Maria, "It is time for you to retire," and take her away from that room.

However, if the parents stop there, they will not have completed addressing the argument. Surely, at some other moment, a more conducive one, after the children have calmed down, they should talk to their children about sharing, love and mutual respect between brothers and sisters. They should talk to them about how great a gift it is to have siblings, how much more easily they can face difficulties if they stay united and loved, how fortunate they will be in their lives if there is love, communication, solidarity and respect between them. This will be the repository of their values and feelings.

Boys and Girls

Parents tend to advise and point to a certain way of behaviour which is different for girls and boys. Words such as "boys don't cry" or "girls don't play with boyish toys" make their development and their journey through life a difficult one as, both adults, man and woman, will be called to equally succeed, not only during their education, but also in their relationships, their professional life and later on, as parents. During this stage our children go through, such behaviour blocks the mechanisms of expressing their personalities, a very important element for them while they try to shape the image of their own selves, apart from us.

Hence, we should let the girl and the boy express their feelings openly and adopt elements from both parents. Anyhow, during their puberty, they reject many of the lessons learnt while they adopt behaviours that better express them in their effort to shape their own personality.

Sex Education

Sex education is amongst the many issues that concern a parent. How are they going to talk to or answer the questions posed by their son or daughter?

Since childbirth and up until the age of 10, a child tries to express its sexuality to its parents, according to its gender. The parents must be very cautious during that period of their child's life as it is a landmark for their maturity and psychosexual development. At a very young age, a child will start exploring its body and touching its genitalia. Parents shouldn't panic or worry. It is a time of searching and exploration.

From the age of six and up until the age of twelve, children go through psychosexual development. During this time, the male children disassociate themselves from the female ones and as a result, they create same-sex groups while later on, when the groups become bigger in size, they 'split', so, one sex approaches the other while attracting one another. This attraction will become sexual attraction during adolescence.

At a very early age, children tend to ask how they came into the world. The parents regulate their response according to the child's age. Their answer must be simple and sincere. "Daddy very lovingly planted his seed into mummy's tummy and that's how you were born." There are books with simple sketches that describe how parents reach the point of having their baby.

Also, their questions concern the bodily differences between girls and boys. Here, as well, we should talk to them simply with the aid of books that demonstrate the anatomical differences between the two sexes.

The ideal age for sexually educating children is during the last grades of primary school because, as we will see further down, the sexual feeling has not developed yet. Asking for details about what they hear all around them, they expect to learn from us everything that concerns the relationship between the two sexes, the sexual act and other relevant questions. That sort of behaviour requires high levels of trust and a good relationship between the children and their parents. Thus, they will not go running for answers to others, who might be malevolent and dangerous.

We should be prepared for these questions and not avoid answering them because if we do, we give the impression that this is something unacceptable, dirty and forbidden. Consequently, we will create a bad image about their body and so, they will learn not to take care of it, not to love it, something that will create a complex in their future sexual life.

Of course you must be wondering what a person could possibly say or describe to a young child! The best reaction is to not go into detail, to use simple words and first connect human interactions with positive feelings, such as love and caring, which justify what we are trying to explain. In this way, we lead them to positive thinking concerning all human interactions and functions and, basically, we cultivate an emotional background behind every relationship.

Let us not forget that we are the best example for our children and every single day, through the way we treat our relationship as companions (showing honest concern, acts of love and care toward one another), we prove to them that there is truth to back up our words.

CHILD ABUSE – CHILD NEGLECT

We say that a child is abused or neglected when one or more adults that are responsible for their care cause or allow bodily harm or deprivation to such an extent that it causes severe physical, mental, emotional or social disorders in the child, or even leads to death.

We highlight the fact that people attending to a child can be – other than the parents – relatives, institution staff, teachers, baby nurses and so on.

The forms of abuse are:

- *Physical*. A blow by hand or using an object, pinching, hair pulling, bites, kicks, inappropriate methods of discipline for a child.

- *Emotional*. It involves verbal, mostly, behaviour that damages the psychological-emotional development of a child. Such behaviour can be yelling, negative characterisations, the lack of love and affection, the creation of guilt, humiliation, threats of abandonment or violence.

- *Sexual*. Refers to any kind of behaviour that will result in the sexual arousal of an adult.

- *Neglect and exposure to danger*. It refers to the deprivation of a child of basic and necessary articles for its life and its healthy upbringing. Such needs can be nourishment, clothing, housing, a clean and healthy environment, health care, education.

- *Exploitation*. It refers to the exploitation of a child for financial gain, mainly to benefit an adult. Child labour, beggary, or child prostitution are all forms of exploitation.

The most important consequences of abuse are on the *child's mental health*. An abused child shows difficulty adjusting to a daily routine and has behavioural problems. It fears for its own and others' safety and finds it immensely difficult to develop a sense of trust. It often shows signs of post-traumatic stress, sleep disorders, disorders of behaviour or personality development.

At school, *it isolates itself from its fellow students* and *it develops a sense of shame*; it has a tendency to be secretive and its performance declines due to the appearance of learning disorders. This child has high levels of anxiety; it constantly feels fear and has problems sleeping while also having frequent nightmares. It feels there is no hope, that no one can help and that the situation will never change.

How can we, the parents, function as a protective shield against these possibilities?

We should always discuss and inform the children from a very young age – without scaring them or creating panic – concerning the odd behaviour that they might come up against, and the way they could handle everything.

Of course, the good relationship between our children and us should be a given so that they feel at ease talking with us freely without hesitating. We should inform them that when someone asks them to keep a secret, they should think whether it is a bad or a good secret and to make it clear that: "A good secret is one that makes you smile and feel happy while, on the contrary, a bad secret is one that makes you feel bad or worried. The only way to feel good is to share the secret with an adult whom you can trust. If, for example, someone touches you in a manner that will make you feel bad, this is a bad act and you should ask an adult for help. It is not appropriate for someone to ask you to keep such a bad secret! You should talk to an adult." (Mallinos – Moore Jennifer, 2006a)

When our child tells us something that happened to it, we should not panic and, in no case, should we make the child feel guilty. If, for some reason, we cannot address the problem ourselves, we should ask a professional for help.

LOSS OF LOVED ONES

Children should be informed that life is a cycle: we are born, we live and eventually we die. The same applies for everyone, even our pets.

It is true that children form greater emotional bonds with the important people in their lives and the same goes for their pets.

When the inevitable happens, children experience strong emotions as they feel that the love and security that they were getting from the person that has passed away is also lost. After such events, children often show different kinds of emotions, such as the behaviour of younger children; they wet their beds or feel guilty due to their conduct, e.g. "If I were more obedient, mum wouldn't have got ill." Also, they might refuse to attend school or they may not want to hang out with their peers.

If we observe such behaviour, we should face them calmly and steadily by explaining the truth to the child. We should not try to hide the death of a loved one by using expressions such as "Grandpa is gone" or

"Mum went on a long trip". In this way, the child will never be able to believe that the departure is definite and irreversible and it will always expect its beloved person to return.

We ought to encourage our children to express their sadness, their anger, their fears or even their guilt because, in this way, we will be able to explain that the loss of that specific person was not caused by something the child did or didn't do and hence, they should not feel responsible for it.

We could prompt them to retain all the happy moments they had shared with the deceased loved one, either through photographs or by talking about them, but without clinging to them. Of course, our preparation is the key, since we, ourselves, first need to be in a position to confront the situation within us so as to be in a position to also convince our child.

MULTIPLE ROLES AND CONFLICTS

As members of a family, we are sometimes called upon to fulfil multiple roles; being the mother, the father, the companion, the worker, roles that tend to satisfy different needs but, when other situations occur, such as lack of time or financial difficulties, these roles are in conflict and we usually find ourselves in the difficult position of having to put aside either our own needs or the needs of our children or of our spouses.

We should stress the fact that the constant neglect of those roles brings about crucial empty places in our lives, which, unfortunately, become evident after quite a few years and might lead to bigger empty places that are irreversible.

To a great extent, this has to do with the time limits we force upon ourselves during our daily schedule and hence, finding the necessary time to devote to ourselves so that we can read a newspaper, go out for a walk, meet with a friend, talk to our partner. If, for example, we spend too much time on housecleaning, something that usually creates tension in others, or we spend too much time at work so as to, supposedly, offer more economic comfort, this usually happens so as to fill up an emotional or communicational void.

We should not forget that when we are happy and 'fulfilled', we are capable of offering our children a higher quality of life.

Ensuring Free Time for Our Children

Free time, for a child, is very important, not only for the child itself but also for its parents, its relatives and its close social surroundings.

Its purpose is:

1. To contribute to personal happiness

2. Replenish physical and psychological strength

3. To decompress

4. To entertain

5. To give a creative outlet

6. To help emotional development

7. To socialise

8. To create interests.

The goals mentioned are fulfilled when the family makes sure to have common free time for all its members, time to socialise, interact, play, rest, travel, go on short trips, see relatives, have hobbies and so on.

By ensuring free time, opportunities are given for the development of the child's creativity through music, the cinema, the theatre, painting, reading and other activities.

Making good use of free time plays a valuable role in a child's progress in school and, when finding common free time is a family concern, relationships become stronger and the family functions like an emotionally well-oiled machine.

Many parents tend to get frightened and troubled as to how they can make time. In order for them to find it, they should change some of their time-consuming activities. They should be the ones to make changes, given the fact that time does not change and a day will always last for 24 hours.

Correct time management and programming will help the parents have time for their children. Hence, the children will also learn how to programme their daily routine.

It would be wise if a daily schedule is made with the help of all family members and is then posted at a visible spot inside the house so that everyone can try to follow it. It is our children's dream to have as much free time as possible. However, parents tend to do the exact opposite. They overburden them with a thousand different activities, which is sometimes due to their own unfulfilled past desires.

Children need more time for outdoor activities. They want to play with water, dirt, mud. They need to lie on the grass, play with their pets, walk with their parents in the countryside, talk, feel nature and discover its magic, explore. Parents should play with their children instead of watching them from afar. They could take them to the theatre, the cinema, museums and after being full of experiences, they can discuss everything they have seen.

All this helps with the child's mental state. A child cannot be deprived of its playtime because of an overburdened schedule. According to psychologist, Dr Jack Wetter, "children that are too pressured might not be able to express their emotions, but the symptoms are there. They become moody or suffer from aches and pains; they cannot sleep or feel worried when they lose contact with their friends".

Also, children need ample time to sleep and rest. A child's sleep, and more importantly a student's, should not last for less than 9 hours, according to the National Sleep Institution, so that it can have enough energy and be ready for school.

THE INTERNET

Nowadays, the Internet has become an important part of our children's lives and there are plenty of times when they spend too much time on it, with all the negative consequences that it may bring.

We could not possibly forbid its use. However, we can keep the timing under control. For children under the age of 12, internet use should be done under close parental supervision because it is a very tender and innocent age for them. The parents must inform their children about the safe use of the internet without, however, causing them fear and a sense of mystery that might actually make them want to secretly surf the web. It would be good if we could point out that the internet is used mainly to search for information and that not everything that is presented to them through the internet is real. After you create a relationship of trust between you and your child, then the child will have nothing to fear and it will indeed talk to its parents if something does not look right.

Until the child reaches adolescence, it would be good for the computer to be in a visible spot so that we can keep an eye on the child, e.g.

the living room. We should have protection filters installed and strictly enforce the time limits of computer use which, for children aged 4 to 6, can be 20 – 30 minutes, always under our supervision, for children aged 7 to 9, it can be 30 minutes and a little while longer during the weekends, always after parental permission, and children aged 9 – 11 can use the computer when they need it for school projects for no more than one and a half hours – always with a parent supervising.

Besides, primary school children come into contact with computers at school and learn, little by little, that they should use technology as a tool to gain knowledge and to make their lives easier and not so that they can waste free and creative time. It depends on us, therefore, to keep repeating this piece of advice every chance we get during our conversations with our children.

However, so as to balance the child's needs, we can make sure they meet their friends face-to-face and not chat with them online.

We should motivate our children to take up activities such as sports, scouting, etc.

We should explain to them that the internet can be a fantastic tool that brings the most remote places of the planet into our own home and offers us a plethora of information, but also hides many unimaginable dangers. That is why they should develop critical thinking when it comes to what they read or see when they are online. You should stress that you are always there for them in case someone bothers them or if they get scared by something. It would be wise not to scold them in such cases so as to encourage them to consult us without any hesitation.

As far as we can, we should make sure that our child only chats with the friends they have met face-to-face and not with strangers, not even friends of people they know, until their identity can be proven. Also, they should not send photos or videos for which they might later regret having shared and feel bad because they will have exposed themselves or others.

If you need to report a crime, do not hesitate to contact the *Electronic Crime Unit* or the police.

THE BROKEN FAMILY

It is true that, nowadays, families change form more frequently than in the past. Couples tend to get divorced more easily for several reasons and divorce is on the rise. More often than not, it is better for a couple to separate than to live a life full of conflict and, sometimes, hatred.

If the couple does not have children, things are much simpler, even though getting divorced never comes without pain. If there are children, then the painful consequences pass on to the children. Many believe that the children would feel better after the separation as they would not have to deal with their parent's arguments anymore. In reality, though, children rarely feel this way.

For the parents, the divorce can bring relief but things are not the same for the children, even when they encourage their parents toward it. The reason why this happens is that the children, as opposed to their parents, do not believe their lives will become better. They believe that the divorce is a loss for them.

While having these thoughts we wonder: Would it be better for the parents to stay together despite the disagreements and the conflicts, for the sake of their children? The answer is not an easy one since research specialists hold differing opinions. One opinion is that it is

better for the children to have a problematic marriage than a divorce, even if the divorce comes with excellent terms. Meaning, "everything but a divorce", according to psychiatrist Judith Wallerstein.

Another opinion (given to us by researcher, George Menahem) is that physical illnesses and psychological disturbances are far greater in individuals who had to live with parents who had problems in their relationship. Consequently, based on this opinion, it would be best for the couple to get divorced.

Hence, what damages the child the most is not the divorce itself but the conflicts between the parents.

We can see that there is no solid answer. What we can say is that:

    a. if the child is properly informed by both parents early on about the causes of their divorce and they ensure the child that it is in no way to blame;

    b. if the parents, convincingly, tell their child that both of them will stand by its side with the same love and care;

    c. if the parents, after the divorce, do not continue to argue in front of their children;

    d. if the parents do not use their child to blame one another;

    e. if the parents find ample time to spend with their child;

    f. if both parents talk to their child about the changes that will occur after the divorce, e.g. which parent it will be living with from then on, when it will be able to see the other parent, how they are going to share the time during holidays and vacationing,

then the child will experience its parents' divorce with fewer problems, less fear, fewer consequences and with a greater feeling of safety and psychological balance. So, it will feel respected and valued, something that a child much desires and needs. We should not forget that it is very important for a child to feel that both its parents are close to it emotionally, so that it can have trust and be able to discuss its concerns and the new feelings that will surface with them, without feeling it is a burden to its parents.

Is a child's school performance influenced by its parents' divorce?

The answer is neither a yes nor a no because the studies that have been conducted on the subject do not provide us with a clear answer. In order for us to have the right answer, we should investigate whether the child's declining school performance is due to the divorce or the conflicts before the divorce and due to the way their family had been functioning.

Finally, it is certain that some children will have difficulties at school after the divorce if the parents do not continue to care about their progress there, with the same level of interest they had before, as far as the child's progress is concerned (taking part in school festivities, parent-teacher meetings, grades, timely morning arrival). The level and duration of difficulties a child will be called upon to face during its school years depends on its parents' behaviour and choices.

SINGLE-PARENT FAMILIES

Within the single-parent families or the families where the two parents are alienated or even when one of them is forced to live far away due to work, the roles of mother and father are taken on by only one of the parents. That specific role creates additional obligations and burdens the parent with more responsibilities.

How is the child's life affected under these circumstances? When one of the parents is away, the child feels insecure, starts having phobias and, in many cases, it exhibits violent behaviour. Additionally, it feels bad when it is among other children that have only good things to say about their parents – a parent who is absent in this child's case. When the child is a girl and lives with the mother, it has the role model of a mother – woman. But when it is a boy living with its mother, then the male role model is absent. In that case, the child should have contact with close relatives (e.g. uncle, cousin, grandfather, etc.) so that it can have a male role model. The same goes for a father who is raising a daughter; he should make sure the girl has contact with the female members of the extended family.

❀   ❀

In some cases, children are raised by their grandparents or mostly their grandmother. The grandmother will give them love, care and open arms. Grandparents are of a different age compared to the child's parents and they do not share the same ideas. What they do have though is ample experience. They set the boundaries and the terms according to what they have learnt. Children cannot accept those terms because they live in a different time, with different ethics and customs. In these situations, the grandparents should understand the children, and while putting aside their ego, they should talk to them and explain their own difficulties with love and sincerity.

When a third party is called to act as a parent, apart from the grandparents, such as an uncle or an aunt, then things become more complicated and the problems are plenty and difficult; of course there are always some exceptions to the rule. However, the difficulties on both sides are plenty. Misunderstandings are frequent, complaints are many, conflicts are inevitable.

In order to face this situation with as little negative influence on the child as possible and also, so that the communication can become more effective, they should have a sincere discussion with the children in which they should inform them of their own anxiety, their fears, their concerns and their responsibilities as far as they are concerned.

Mainly though, they should inform them of the love and interest they have toward them. They should open their arms and make them feel safe and the warmth of the family. They should try to offer the children as much as possible; what every child would expect from their parents. They should help the children lessen the feeling of missing their parents, regardless how hard it is for them and the children. They should be more patient with them than they would be with their very own children.

CHAPTER 2

Education: Preparing the Ground

The education of the young resembles the art of potters. Just like them, when the clay is still fresh, they can form it as they wish and give it any shape they like, but, when it dries out there is nothing more they can do; the same applies to people that have not been educated persistently and correctly during their youth; no correction can be made to their character.

Diogenes

(Triantafillidi, 2010, p.62)

AS WE WILL SEE BELOW, the responsibility of a child's education falls on the parents; however, the fruits of their labour, the satisfaction, the pride and the feeling of fulfilment are also theirs to enjoy throughout their entire life.

HOW TO BECOME BETTER PARENTS

Becoming better parents demands that we be better people. We should look inwards and recognise or improve our skills and those characteristics that will help us succeed in providing the most effective education for our children.

All parents wish to raise happy, responsible children, who are bright students and have good manners. At the same time, however, we do not know how to achieve these goals. So, what is needed?

CULTIVATING OUR EMOTIONAL INTELLIGENCE

Most of the analyses that are presented below are based on the degree of growth of *emotional intelligence* and *emotional education* initially of the parents, so that they can, in turn, become able to apply these ideas in the education of their children. The parents who want to raise emotionally intelligent children should, first and foremost, learn how to manage their own emotions and realise that this will affect the way their own children face their emotions.

The emotional education of parents is an art and is based on the deeper sentiments of love and empathy toward our children. Nevertheless, that does not mean that all parents who love their children can also be their emotional 'mentors'; *only those who acknowledge their feelings can constructively handle certain techniques of active listening and problem solving, not only in their own relationships but also in the relationship they have with their children.*

More specifically, the ability to perceive, express and handle emotions, self-control, empathy, quality communication, an assertive attitude, personal responsibility, self-awareness are the skills that make up emotional intelligence within the emotional interactions of children in the family and at school.

As empathic parents, when we see our children sad and upset, we can imagine ourselves being in their shoes and feel their pain. When we convey this personal, emotional understanding, we show faith in their experiences and we help them calm down. Empathy allows children to regard their parents as allies and not as enemies.

Imagine growing up in a family that had empathic understanding as its goal:

If you were to say you had had an argument with your best friend at school, your mother would ask you about how it had happened, how it had made you feel and if she could help you find a solution.

If there had been a misunderstanding between you and your teacher, your parents wouldn't immediately side with the teacher. They would carefully listen to your side of the story and they would believe you because they trust you and they know you're telling the truth.

If your younger brother ruined the toy collection you loved so much, your mother would hug you and tell you she understood why you were upset. You really loved those toys and you have been collecting them with great care.

That is how empathy works. When we seek to understand our children's experiences, we help them understand they have someone to support them. We are on their side. We avoid judging them, doubting them, minimising the intensity of their feelings: hence, they let us enter their world. They tell us how they feel, they express their opinion, their motives become clear and that leads to greater understanding. Our children start to trust us. So, they have no need to 'act out' in order to draw our attention.

Because we do not disapprove of our children's feelings, there are fewer conflicts within the family. Children are not scolded because they cried or because they expressed their anger. But, we also set boundaries and make clear what behaviour is acceptable and what behaviour is not. When children know the rules and understand the consequences of breaking them, then they are less likely to behave badly.

This method of education creates stronger emotional bonds between the parents and the children and, as a result, children respond better to their parents' wishes. They wish to please them and not disappoint them. And hence, it is more likely that the day will come when they will truly want to hear their parents' advice.

The parents who apply an empathic parental style and, as a result, appreciate the power and the purpose of feelings in life, are not afraid to express themselves in front of their children; they believe they can constructively express their anger, sadness or fear and, in so doing, serve as role models for their children.

A child that observes its parents conversing in a heated manner but later sees them solve their differences in a friendly way learns valuable lessons on how we resolve conflicts and about the strength of relationships that are based on love.

The child that sees its parents grieving over the death of a grandparent can learn valuable lessons on how people should cope with pain and despair. This is especially true of situations where adults love and support one another by offering love and understanding. The child learns that sharing sadness leads to a higher level of intimacy and bonding.

A certain degree of patience and creativity is needed for emotional education to succeed. This means that parents should be relatively undistracted and calm to act properly. Also, the children should be developmentally mature enough to be receptive to such teachings. From early childhood (over the age of four) children have the potential to develop skills to cope with their emotions.

There are, of course, situations in which the application of emotional education should be postponed. This happens when:

- PARENTS ARE PRESSED FOR TIME

Modern families are always in a hurry. We run around trying to get to the nursery school on time, to school, to work. Such moments are not suitable for the application of emotional education, given the fact that it is a process that requires certain steps be made in the right order.

- THERE IS AN AUDIENCE

We should apply emotional education when we are alone with our child, face-to-face, without the presence of other family members, friends or relatives. This way parents avoid putting the child on the spot. Besides, both the parents and the child will feel more comfortable asking and answering questions when it is just the two of them. This is very important for families that have to deal with sibling rivalry.

- PARENTS ARE UPSET OR TIRED

Intense anger or exhaustion can hinder our ability to think clearly and to communicate in the most effective way. In such cases, parents should postpone the emotional education until they are rested and feel emotionally ready. In this way, they will have greater benefits.

- PARENTS HAVE TO DEAL WITH SERIOUS ISSUES OF MISCONDUCT

Sometimes we are forced to impose some form of discipline that goes beyond simply setting limits. If a child's actions come into direct conflict with our moral code, we will need to express our disapproval. At that moment, the right thing to do would be to express exactly what we feel concerning the child's actions, why we think they are wrong and why we feel so bad. And it is also good to talk about our emotions of anger and disappointment (without humiliating the child) as well as our values.

- A CHILD IS 'PRETENDING' TO EXPERIENCE A FEELING
SO AS TO 'MANIPULATE' THE PARENTS

The moment our child tries to manipulate us by using its feelings, any effort we make to engage in a process of empathic listening or provide emotional education is fruitless. That is the moment when parents should make it clear to the child that its actions will have no effect whatsoever on their decision.

As we have already said, emotional education is not some sort of magic potion that eliminates family tensions and conflicts or the need to set boundaries. It can, however, help us approach our children. It cultivates the ground for teamwork where all the problems can be solved jointly. Our children learn that they can disclose their feelings because they know we will not judge them, nor will we hurt their feelings.

Growing up, they will not experience the feeling that can be summed up in this phrase: "I loved my father but I was never able to truly talk to him." When our children are faced with a problem, they will turn to us because they know that we will offer them something more than general advice and rules. They know that we will listen carefully to their souls.

However, the true beauty of emotional education is that its results last throughout adolescence. By then, the children will have embraced our values and they will reap the rewards of emotional intelligence. They will know how to concentrate, how to act, how to face their peers, how to handle their intense emotions.

Research conducted by John Gottman and Daniel Goleman has shown that children that are guided emotionally perform better at school, are healthier and have better relationships with their peers. They display fewer behavioural problems and they can easily overcome experiences that cause stress.

Now let's look at the value of applying emotional intelligence in the educational system, starting from the very beginning, nursery school. The Constitution of Greece states that "the purpose of education is to contribute to the whole, harmonious and balanced development of the intellectual and psychosomatic strengths of students..." During the past few years, education has focused on creating people with a satisfactory level of knowledge, advanced cognitive abilities and emotional skills.

The type of education that is not confined to the acquisition and enhancement of cognitive skills but also emphasises the emotional development of students' personality has been adopted by many modern pedagogical institutes. Emotional skills as behavioural factors are subjects that are taught. They are considered useful because by acquiring them children gain greater self-esteem, they improve their communicative and learning skills, they recognise and handle their emotions and, they are also taught how to cope with everyday problems. Obviously, emotional education is not solely the responsibility of parents but also of schools: the teachers who are interested in developing children's emotional competency and choose alternative ways of teaching so as to win their students over, especially the difficult ones. Besides, higher emotional development is linked to better academic performance. The two are closely interrelated. (Gottman, 2011)

REMAINING TRUE TO OUR GOALS

It is very important to always focus on the result we want to achieve and to be consistent concerning the procedures we follow so as to succeed. Therefore, it is very important that we first practice certain techniques and ways of applying behaviour we wish our children to adopt. How much do we personally believe that we are going to do what we say we'll do? How consistent are we in applying these principles because we truly believe that they will benefit our child?

So, we focus on the ultimate goal, which is to do what's best for our child. If, for example, we truly believe and want our children to be healthy throughout their entire life (our goal), we should make sure they adopt proper eating habits starting from a very young age and consistently apply the rules of healthy eating at home. Thus, by setting a good example, we instil these habits in our children who think of them as given. While, on the other hand, if we want to do this but do not really believe in it ourselves, we will be vulnerable and unable to resist every temptation that comes our way and as a result, we will not be able to apply anything correctly.

MAINTAINING A GOOD RELATIONSHIP WITH OUR CHILD

Nothing is of greater importance than having a good relationship with our child, and other people as well. If there is a good relationship then everything can improve and everything can be corrected.

Good relationships serve as 'lifesavers' when dealing with difficult and unexpected behaviour. And when parents have a good relationship with their children, they do not wish to put them at risk because of an argument or a problem. The same goes for children, who deep down inside do not wish to upset their parents. (P. Regoukos, Parenting school, 2001)

COMMUNICATING SUBSTANTIALLY WITH OUR CHILD

The communication between us and our children must be on equal terms, meaning, we should treat them with respect, as unique personalities – according to the skills they have developed – and we should never underestimate them. Children simply want us to listen to them, to take them seriously, to love them and accept them unconditionally. We should listen more than we talk. That's why we have two ears but only one mouth. We should listen for the deeper meaning hidden behind our children's words and try to understand their emotional state.

We should develop our *active listening skills*. We should tell them we understand how they feel and encourage them to find solutions to their problems, but we should discretely stay on as listeners that will support them in their efforts. We ought to use body language, to speak with our eyes and physical contact. We must smile when we need to and remain focused on what they are telling us. This way, we reinforce the child's sense of self-esteem and self-respect. The message the child will receive is: "I love you enough to listen to you."

BEING RELIABLE AND CONSISTENT

Being reliable means, 'I do what I promise to do.' If we promise our child something, we should keep our promise or we will feel its disapproval. Mum says something and then she takes it back. The major factor that causes the most serious disciplinary problems in children is inconsistent parental behaviour. If the rules we make for our children change unpredictably from one day to the next or if we don't apply them consistently then our child's bad behaviour is our own fault, not the child's. If, for example, our child is four years old and we have set a rule that states that they should pick up their toys when they finish playing, it would not be right to ask them to do that only when we feel like tidying the house, but we should make sure the rule is applied *every single time they finish playing*.

Usually, parents become inconsistent without noticing it. If we are having trouble disciplining our child, the first thing we ought to do is question if the actual problem is our own inconsistency. Let us check that possibility before we come up with other explanations.

Accepting Our Child Unconditionally

One of the most important building blocks in our relationship with our child is our unconditional acceptance. Children who grow up feeling unconditional acceptance from their parents are more likely to have a better sense of their personal worth. They are more likely to feel certainty within their relationship with their parents. Unconditional acceptance cultivates self-esteem and self-perception.

Children growing up in such an environment are more likely to get a sense of their true worth because others will accept them for what they truly are and not for what they do, what they have or what they look like. Thus, they feel important, that they matter and that they are worthy of their parent's esteem.

Being Careful Parents

Children come into this world ready to mimic their parents' behaviour. There is nothing the parents can do to stop this from happening. This ability children have to mimic adults is so powerful that scientists now believe that it played a crucial role in the evolution of the human species. For example, if we take an infant of a few months and hold it facing us, it will mimic any facial expression we make. If we stick our tongue out, it will do the same. In fact, a child's ability to learn through observation precedes their ability to learn from other people's teachings.

Parents do not always perceive the subtle messages their children convey to them through their actions and their emotions. If, for example, the child sees its parents solving their problems by yelling and screaming or by verbally abusing each other, it will assume that the best way to deal with a problem is to have heated arguments with others. If, however, we rarely raise our voice then our child is likely to use similar tactics when dealing with other people.

Our children's desire to take after their mother or father when they are older is very powerful – one could say it's innate. The truth is that they constantly observe us, not just inside the house but outside as well. They watch us while we wait in queues, when we order food at the restaurant, the way we react when someone comments (especially negatively) on our driving skills, when we talk with other parents at school or when we have a carefree discussion with fellow passengers at the bus stop or the airport. If we are civil, polite, friendly, or if we apologise for something we did to a fellow citizen, our child will most likely do the same. The child learns how to communicate with other people by observing its parents.

Of course, this does not mean that our children become our exact replicas because during their adolescence they are also influenced by their peers, other members of the family or by the media. Yet, they observe their parents more than anyone else and with greater attention, especially during their formative years. That is why, in the presence of our children, we should not behave in a manner that does not comply with the proper education of our child.

LEARNING FROM OUR MISTAKES

We, as parents, have all made mistakes. When we are tired and pressed for time, we do not communicate with our child effectively. Sometimes, when we feel exhausted and we have no more strength, we cannot impose the rules we have set and so we become too lenient, while when we are moody, we become too strict. When we make a mistake, we should become aware of it, seek its cause and correct it.

Our child will not be permanently traumatised if we lose our temper once or if it sees us arguing with our spouse. The important thing, though, is that when we make a mistake, we should admit it to our spouse and our child and do it in such a way that the child will understand. If we tell the child "I'm sorry I yelled at you before, it was because I had a very rough day today" or "I was thinking of the talk we had yesterday and I think you were probably right", then the child is likely to show respect in the future toward our views. At the same time, we convey the message that when we hurt someone it is good to apologise.

At this point, it would be advisable for parents to get to know themselves and to discover their vulnerabilities. Under what circumstances do they make mistakes they later regret? Usually, when we are pressed for time, we act hastily and may lose our temper. If that is the case, meaning when we are in a state of panic, we should learn to avoid making important decisions. If, for example, our child asks us for permission to go on a field trip with the school and it is in the morning when we are in a hurry to get to work on time, then, the best answer would be, "I would like some time to think about it – let's talk about it later." We should not give in unless it is absolutely necessary, e.g. if the field trip is on that very same day. However, it is important to explain to our child that early morning is not the best time to make such decisions and also suggest that next time they should talk to you about it the day before.

Loving Our Children Unconditionally

Often, in the name of love, we greatly violate a child's personality because we give our love with conditions attached: "I will love you if you get good marks"; "I will love you if you are the way I want you to be". It is difficult to find people who simply say, "I love you". There are many children who were traumatised because their parents were too busy, too selfish or too concerned with their own needs to provide them with love. Unfortunately, these children, when they become adults, cannot give love to their children or their partners.

We often hear that parents spoil their children by loving them too much. That is usually the consequence when we offer our child objects, promises and expectations instead of love. Parents harm their children by not setting boundaries for them, when they have low expectations of them so that they can appear good, or when they use toys, food or gifts as a substitute for true affection or attention.

When we treat our children with real affection, interest and care, our love towards them can never be a hindrance to their healthy psychosocial development. We should remind them that they are our never-ending source of happiness. We should tell them how special they are to us and treat them as unique individuals.

When children feel sincerely loved, they develop a strong sense of security and confidence and so they become less demanding. Let us not forget that the healthier adults, adults who can express their love toward others, are those who have received the selfless, honest and unconditional love of their parents.

REWARDING OUR CHILD'S EFFORTS AND ACCOMPLISHMENTS

A positive attitude is one of the greatest gifts we can give our children. Let's try praising them for their behaviour and actions, showing them that we appreciate them for what they are and what they do. We should reward them when they accomplish certain goals. Their sense of personal strength is all the more reinforced and, in this way, we help them achieve even greater goals.

When we praise our child, we should focus on *the effort*, not necessarily on the result. Much too often, we give too much credit to the result without recognising how hard it is to get there. By praising their efforts, we encourage the child to set new goals and struggle to achieve them, since what matters and what defines the final outcome is indeed the effort, the 'journey' and not the destination.

It would be best to avoid compliments such as, "You did well, *but...*" It's best to avoid labelling when the child does something we do not like and to give specific instructions as to what exactly they should have done instead.

Child psychologist Dimitris Karagiannis advises, "We should praise their talents, their strengths, without adding the word 'but'. When their parents tell them what is good, they put the word 'but' next to it. You're smart but you don't study enough... Therefore, the words 'smart', 'good', 'pretty', 'earnest' lose their meaning and all we have left is the word 'but', which is what is used to confirm their weaknesses. Situations can be inspirational. What we have to do is inspire our child; we shouldn't highlight their mistakes but we can guide them in the direction we want by setting the example."

Children's achievements should be individually assessed. However, if there were a need to compare our children to something, then the best way to do this would be to compare them to their past performance and not the performance of another child or other children. It is much better to say, "This time you threw the ball better than ever!" than "You threw the ball better than the other children". In any case, we should avoid intensifying competition among children because it already exists in schools or in other activities.

On numerous occasions, parents refer to another child's academic performance or other behaviour, thinking that this will encourage their children to achieve better results. This is like inflating a balloon – we try with patience and difficulty to inflate it so that it becomes shiny and beautiful, without realising how easily and quickly it can burst. The same happens when we compare children. They try to achieve the best result but burst internally, and that is a shame. Why are all the children's strengths taken for granted while we find it necessary to emphasise all their weaknesses?

On the contrary, we can tell children how much we admire what they have succeeded in doing. For example, we can praise our child for learning to read a word correctly or managing to complete a difficult homework assignment. We should find the time to look at and admire what the child has done and show him how impressed we are. When work and effort are praised, we show the child the value of hard work in achieving a goal.

If, on the other hand, the child has not done well and is disappointed, we should encourage him by discovering ways that will help him improve next time. When the child is young – seven or eight years of age – it greatly helps to stress the great effort that he has put into succeeding. It is wise to avoid criticism since our child probably already feels bad without our saying anything. Nor should we lie to the child that it has supposedly done well, because unjustified praise reduces the value of justified praise.

How to Encourage our Child

We encourage our child when we inspire courage and reinforce the child's motivation to try. How can this be accomplished? This can be done by focusing our attention on the child's strengths and by building self-confidence and self-esteem. In this way, we also help the child overcome its fears and inhibitions and help it believe it can succeed.

Encouragement is based on acceptance. Parents who encourage their children accept them for what they are and cultivate positive expectations. They discover their child's interests and encourage it to develop them. Courage is the opposite of fear. It builds self-confidence and faith in personal strengths. If the child turns its attention to what it can do, it is encouraged; however, if it focuses on what it cannot do, it becomes disappointed.

The first step is to direct the child towards setting realistic goals, from improving its grades or learning a musical instrument to whatever is within the child's capacity. Regardless of the degree of success, parents should accept any result without pushing for better performance. This is a bit difficult for parents. Let us not forget that when parents push their children – either directly or indirectly – to be more successful, it is as if they are conveying the message: "you are not good enough and you do not reach my expectations!" This rejection leads the child either to indifference or to some sort of reaction.

With encouragement, you increase the prospects of increasing knowledge. If a child is encouraged, it will want to learn more; if it lacks encouragement, the opposite will occur because it believes that when faced with a difficulty it cannot manage. Receiving encouragement enables the child to face the lack of knowledge in a different way. It will try to learn in many ways.

Children possess the ability from within and have the characteristics needed to become proper adults. These characteristics can be transformed into skills when they receive encouragement. A child who is afraid cannot transform opportunity into skill because it fears that it cannot do so.

We encourage our child by recognising and emphasising its strengths and positive behaviour, which also helps it see itself as successful and praiseworthy. This in turn will motivate it to be more cooperative and to adopt positive behaviour, in this way building self-esteem and self-confidence.

We can reinforce this behaviour by saying the following things to our children:

- You are very smart.

- Everything is so beautiful and tidy in your room.

- It was very nice on your part.

- Thank you for not shouting.

- I love you and I love being your mother/father.

- Well done! You work hard.

- Thank you for helping me.

- It doesn't matter. I know you always do the best you can.

- It's good to ask for help, I appreciate your asking me.

- I noticed you shared your things. It was very kind of you to do so.

- Congratulations! You got dressed by yourself today!

- You did a great job!

- Your table manners were excellent today.

- Bravo! I see that you have tidied your room.

How to Inspire

Besides the encouragement that we have to regularly give our children, we can inspire them to adopt a proper way of life. We have to face the problems and difficulties of life as optimistically as we can so that our children can adopt similar behaviour. And as you can very well guess, the only way of achieving this is by setting an example ourselves.

A mother and a father will never succeed in making their child an adult that will get satisfaction from their work and develop if the only thing they do when they get home is complain about how tired they are and about work.

How can parents ask their children to read extracurricular books when they themselves do not read or when there are no books at home? We can think of numerous ways to arouse the child's interest. For example, when our children see us carefully leafing through a book of ancient Greek literature at a book fair or watching a documentary about environmental protection with great interest they will be intrigued to see what it is that attracted our attention so much,– as long as our interest is natural and sincere. Children quickly pick up on these stimuli. We parents are therefore able to become initiators of ideas and situations.

SETTING RULES AND LIMITS

All parents "transfer" their own parents' perceptions and values to their children. These are perceptions that have to do with the basic values of life such as honesty, work, education, success, etc. When both parents are geared towards the same values and there is no confusion between them, that is to say, when there is togetherness and similarity in their perceptions and values, they inspire confidence and stability in the child.

With this attitude, it is difficult for the child to impose its own conditions on issues that are our responsibility. This does not mean that we must be rigid in our behaviour; sometimes we have to negotiate so as not to lose contact with the child, while at the same time we should ask all family members to commit to the agreements that have been made.

However, which parents are able to not only set but also apply the rules and limits? Only the ones who truly believe in the usefulness of the rules and limits that they have set for their child. For whatever they say – and how they say it – should convey that they believe in it and that the limits they set are non-negotiable.

Apart from love, which is the most important thing that children need, parents should cultivate and build a structure to set boundaries and define rules that are age-appropriate. Limits and rules make children feel safe.

Imagine how a child would develop if it lived in a house where every day were unpredictable, if it studied whenever it wanted to, if it ate only when hungry, if it made noise while playing, not respecting the family's quiet time, if it lived at a chaotic pace without rules and limits.

The main reason for clearly defining and applying rules is that, as the child grows older, becoming an adolescent and then an adult, these rules will help it develop the ability to control its own behaviour. This future ability stems from the control that we as parents exercise now. Over time, the external control will transform into internal control, i.e. when the child (adolescent-adult) will be able to exercise control over itself.

The reason why a six-year old child brushes his teeth every night before going to bed, whether his parents see him or not, is that he established this rule-habit when he was four.

The reason why a nine-year old child quietly sits at the dining table while dining at a friend's house and asks for permission before getting up is that this habit was established at his house.

The reason why a thirteen-year old child hands in his homework on time is that when he was in primary school, his parents checked to see that homework was completed every night and noted the importance of this responsibility.

Depending on the child's age and the extent to which he understands the situation, it is of vital importance to explain why we have to apply such limitations, so that the child does not feel coerced into implementing them but does so willingly. Only in this way can we make sure our children will implement these rules in the future. Otherwise, children are capable of doing the exact opposite simply to oppose their parents when not supervised. Such an outcome, however, is futile and no parents would want it. That is, we can explain that when they brush their teeth daily they will always have healthy teeth, fresh breath and a nice smile; in other words, they will be more beautiful.

❦   ❦

On the whole, it is important to explain to children that we have to respect the limits and rules that exist because in so doing we become better people. Of course, the more persuasive we are as parents and the more we set the right example with our own behaviour, the more convinced they are. We cannot demand a particular behaviour from a child when we do the exact opposite. For example, we cannot forbid a child to watch television and force it to go to its room when it can hear the other family members watching television in the living room.

Parents should set limits and rules at each stage of the child's development and monitor their effectiveness while at the same time being strict and fair.

On their part, at every stage of their development, children control their limits by testing their parents. Preschoolers complain about restrictions on television viewing while primary school children complain about having to tidy their room. Teenagers complain about everything.

Of course, it is certain that children and parents will have differing views as to what is best for them, but parents are wiser, more experienced, have greater foresight and can see the big picture of things.

And this is what it all boils down to...the key to effectively applying and setting limits and rules is for there to be a healthy relationship between parents and children. When good relationships are cultivated, parents can convey the message to their children that rules are imposed and limits set not to show who is in control and who decides, but because these rules derive from the wisdom and good judgment of their parents.

"Clearly, the parents are the important people who are responsible for changing the situation. They form the family context," says child psychiatrist, Dimitris Karagiannis. In the long run, the clearly set roles will foster trust and cooperation. Also, according to the professor, what we say is not so important as how we say it; as the look on our face that accompanies the words... In other words, how parents use body language in a positive way when they talk to their children. In challenging situations, parents usually have an angry, imposing, derogatory and stressful manner so regardless of what words they choose to use, the expression of their eyes and the tone of their voice destroys any positive message. Limits should be set with love and affection, not when we're tired or angry. For example, we should say, 'No, my dear child, no, my sweet, no, no.' (smiling).

❀　　❀

"At that moment, this 'no' is a clear, 'I'm-not-backing-down' but also a clear 'I-love-you'; it means: 'I am simply saying no, I'm not depriving you of anything.' But what do parents usually do? First, they set rules and when their children start nagging, they back down and give in to their children, thus, encouraging their children to nag and training them to grumble."

We see, therefore, that how we set limits and impose rules is equally important as whether we will set limits and enforce rules. That is why, above all, rules have to be fair and reasonable. That is to say, good rules must be age-appropriate and flexible enough to change as the child matures. It is a good idea to re-examine rules, and if they are reasonable and effective, then there is no reason to change them.

In other instances, when a new rule could serve the same purpose as the old one, it need not be significantly changed. For example, if in the past we asked our child to finish his homework before going out to play, now that he is better able to manage his time on his own, we can simply insist that he finish his homework before going to bed and allow him to choose when to do it.

Changing the rules when necessary shows the child that our rules are based on logic and not on our power to decide about everything.

It is just as much our responsibility to change the rules as it is to apply exceptions to the rules.

We should clarify any exceptions to our child and stick to our rules. In no case should rule changes or temporary exceptions be the child's decision. The decision to make an exception is ours and ours alone. Still, we must remember that if we have to make such decisions, we must make them for the right reasons and not because it is easier or more convenient to give in than to remain faithful to our principles.

Even so, conflicts between parents and children are inevitable. We will set rules that our children will not like and we will argue about them. In cases where we might simply impose our power, we may temporarily resolve the dispute in our favour, but the child will feel defeated, which may cause resentment and rebellion in the future.

Simply giving in to the child's wishes is not recommended because in so doing we automatically transfer control to the child, which can prove catastrophic in the short run. For example, our seven-year-old child insists on studying at night before going to bed. Our ten-year-old child insists that he should be the one to decide when it is time to tidy his room.

We should be more lenient only when our child is right or when the issue is trivial to us but important for our child; for example, when it concerns what clothes a pre-teen will wear to a friend's party. To allow our child to make his own choices – rather than impose our own – shows him that we are willing to listen to his views, and in this way, he will be more willing to accept our decisions when we come to a disagreement in the future and we are right.

We must be careful not to set unreasonable rules so that we do not find ourselves in the difficult position of having our authority undermined or feeling bad when the rules are repeatedly violated. At the same time, however, we should be very careful, we should insist on compliance and we should not back down as an easy way out.

❦   ❦

The recommended way to deal with a disagreement about rules with our child (unless it concerns our non-negotiable principles) is to reach a mutual solution to a problem. We can find a better rule that satisfies both. It is better to focus on revising or diversifying the rule rather than on trying to enforce it.

If, for example, our eight-year-old child does not want his breakfast to include milk, we can replace the milk with another dairy product from a list we've made together. It is better for our child to continue getting the necessary proteins through other products than to stop consuming them simply because this rule was imposed.

If our child refuses to put his jacket on before leaving for school, insisting that he wear it despite his objections will only make him take it off all the more quickly as soon as he is out of our range of supervision, and in so doing, he will risk catching a cold. But if we tell him to hold it and put it on when he feels cold, there is a chance he will put it on.

DEFINING OUR NON-NEGOTIABLE PRINCIPLES

Our non-negotiable principles should be those we have set in order to safeguard the health and safety of our children. These, apart from health and safety issues, could also address behavioural issues or a family value, i.e. they are forbidden to take things without asking, to steal, to be disrespectful, and so on. There are no compromises as concerns these principles.

Everything depends on the age of the child and our own value system. For example, a non-negotiable rule for our child of ten may be that it is forbidden to return home from school unsupervised. This rule can later be replaced by one stipulating that the child must always call home after school if it wants to go to a friend's house and call again once it has reached his friend's house. When the child reaches puberty, the non-negotiable rules change and may include a prohibition of alcohol, smoking and drugs. We could make a list of non-negotiable rules, but this list should not be too long.

Violation of Rules and Limits:
Punishment - Reward - Explanation

We always try to explain the necessity of a rule to our children so that it is clear to them why they should follow it. In practice, however, there are always cases in which the rules are violated. If our child does something we do not approve of or that angers us, then:

- We should not act immediately if we are out of control. We should take a deep breath and count to three, and in a strict but calm tone, we can tell our child that we are outraged. We should wait until we have calmed down before we do something about the situation. For example, if the child is seven or eight years old, we can tell him that we are very angry at what he did and that we cannot discuss it at the moment. It is advisable that we don't take too long to calm down. Immediate action is more effective than a delayed one.

- Avoid any form of violence, whether verbal or physical. Do remember that what we want to focus on is the content of the message and not the way we express ourselves. The child should focus on his bad behaviour, and not on our shouting.

- We should disapprove of the child's behaviour and not the child itself. Instead of calling him a liar and wiping out his personality, we should talk about his behaviour. For example, we say, "It was wrong to lie about not doing your math homework yesterday."

- We should prepare what we have to say. Very often, parents impose excessive punishment because they have reacted quickly and impulsively. We must carefully select the words we use and how we express what we have to say.

- We should avoid inflicting harsh punishment. Long-term use of punishment may cause permanent opposition or hostility in the future.

- The punishment should fit each child's temperament. We must carefully consider the child's age, temperament and interests when deciding on which form of punishment is the most appropriate.

- Punishment is effective when it is used consistently. The consistency with which punishment is meted out for bad behaviour is more important than the kind of punishment used. This means we should faithfully implement the imposed punishment. If we give in to the child's pressure when the time for punishment comes and we do not impose it properly, then it has no effect. On the contrary, when we are consistent and our child knows that whenever it behaves badly, punishment will be imposed it will certainly limit and gradually eliminate the occurrence of such behaviour.

- If we want to have the desired result, then punishment must be unpleasant. We do not punish a child for bad behaviour by making him stay in his room where he has everything he needs to enjoy himself.

The basic procedure to follow in such cases is as follows:

1. We clearly state the child's wrongful act: "I have repeatedly told you to wipe your feet before entering the house so as not to fill it with mud."

2. Describe the consequences of this act: "Now we have to mop again."

3. Suggest one or more alternative ways of behaviour: "You can use the mat outside or you can take off your shoes before you enter."

4. State the punishment: "Now please go clean the floor."

5. Express our expectation that this behaviour will not be repeated: " I hope you are more careful next time."

SPENDING QUALITY TIME WITH OUR CHILD

Quality time refers to how we spend time when we are together with our child. It is important to be committed to the child when we do things together. We cannot give it our full attention when we are simultaneously cooking supper or reading documents, emails or our newspaper.

We should spend time with our child when we can really focus our attention on what we are doing together, and not just when we squeeze in some free time between other activities. When the child receives the required attention from its parents, it is less likely to do things to attract our attention.

It is constructive to find time for joint activities in which our children and we have the opportunity to really communicate. How you do this depends on the age of the child and on what he likes and what not. However, whatever the age, surely we can find something that we will enjoy doing together. What counts most is not the activity itself but our willingness to devote to whatever we are doing together.

If we do not do so as prescribed above, the child will understand that we are not participating wholeheartedly in this joint activity and that we are merely doing certain things mechanically.

If you are wondering how much quality time is needed and how much is enough, there is no magical way of calculating the minutes or hours we should devote to our child. The more quality time we spend together, the better it is.

In the case of two children of different ages, we should devote individual time to each child because, quite obviously, the older child will not want to do what the younger child wants to do, and vice versa, or the younger child won't be able to understand the content of conversation with the older child.

RESPECTING OUR CHILD

The key to effective parental behaviour is equality and mutual respect. The basic principle that all families should keep in mind is that all members of the family should – irrespective of whether they are parents or children – live on an equal basis.

Equality means that neither parents nor children are superior to each other. Parents should treat their children as unique individuals depending on the abilities and skills they have developed.

We often wonder if our children respect us enough without wondering if we respect our children enough.

- Are we as kind to our children as we are to others?

- Do we respect their point of view?

- Do we pay attention when they are talking or do we ignore them when we happen to be talking to someone else?

- Do we treat them with kindness?

- Do we strive to make them happy?

Respect is the ideal way to motivate our children to treat not only us but also others like relatives, teachers, friends, etc. with respect. In the long run, it also fosters a willingness to cooperate with others and to resolve problems and conflicts peacefully.

LOVE IS THE FOUNDATION STONE

You may have gotten tired of hearing that parents have to show their children love. Unfortunately, many children grow up without love and the consequences become evident many years later.

Children can't get enough of love; they not only need to hear it, but also to feel it on a daily basis. Physically, love is expressed through touch, hugs, kisses, and friendly pats on the back. Verbally, they should hear it every day.

It is true that as children grow up and reach the end of primary school or high school, they appear to no longer have a need for love. This may be temporary because a transition period begins where they enter other social groups, those of high school, and they begin to compare themselves to classmates and friends. However, this is when they need love more than ever.

Indeed, many parents tend to show less affection to their children as they grow older and when they reach puberty, when they are trying to discover their personal identity and build a good image of themselves. That is when they need love more than ever.

One reason why teenagers turn to sexual relationships is to prove that there is someone who loves them. Therefore, we need to tell them that we love them, to embrace them and to show them our love in any way we can so that they can satisfy this feeling in the family.

Research which has been conducted on neglected, missing or children, who for some reason or other haven't received love or affection, has shown that these children suffer from mental and physical decline that can even result in death. These findings show that children are healthier when they are raised with love, care and affection. Children who grow up without love do not grow up properly, even if their diet is excellent.

In every decade, we see that the time when children reach puberty changes. In the 50s, the average child reached puberty at 14. Now the average age that children reach puberty is 12.

Therefore, because children enter puberty at an increasingly younger age, they are less able to handle the emotional stress that accompanies the changes to the body and therefore have a greater need for emotional support. This emotional support should be given to them by their family.

Let us ask ourselves the following question as often as possible:

"How many times have we embraced our children today?"

And let us never think that we can overdo it with hugs. A child's age or height does not matter. The need for love does not pass with age. There is a surprisingly great force hidden within the small but very important things in life, such as a hug or a nod that says, "I love you." (Steinberg, 2006)

CHAPTER 3

Kindergarten

A CHILD OF THREE TO FIVE YEARS OF AGE is considered a preschooler. At this age, children have begun to socialise not only in the family but also in other institutions. In urban centres, these institutions are the nursery school, which involves the simple care and custody of the child when both parents are absent from home and which, theoretically, a child may attend from an early age; and the kindergarten, which operates as the official provider of preschool education in every advanced country worldwide.

The aim of kindergarten is to help children develop physically, emotionally, mentally and socially within the context of the wider objectives of primary and secondary education.

During early childhood, the intellectual and language development of a child is greatly influenced by the environment and the changes that occur are very rapid. You can easily imagine that at this age, if a child receives positive influences, the results are significant.

According to university textbooks, language development in four- and five-year-olds is surprisingly rapid. Even before the child attends school, the major milestones in language acquisition have already been achieved: articulation has reached maturity (90% of six-year-olds have perfected articulation). They have acquired a vocabulary of about 2,500 words (600 words annually) and they can effectively use all the major variants of simple sentence structures.

Of course, the limits of further language development and improvement are almost infinite. However, if a child does not receive the proper upbringing, the desired interaction with their caregivers, and appropriate stimulation during this critical period, they run the risk of not properly or fully developing their intellectual and language skills, which may later affect social or academic growth and development.

According to the views of both modern Developmental Psychology as well as the Psychology of Learning, the ability of a student to achieve a goal and learn a subject does not depend so much on age and physical maturity as on previous school and extracurricular experiences. (Kapsalis & Vrettos, 1997)

It is common knowledge that not all children possess the skills they need to meet the demands of kindergarten to the same degree. There are great differences between them due to social as well as cultural factors. All the children live in different family environments and may not speak the same language. The role of kindergarten here is countervailing, that is to say, it tries to minimise the differences that exist between children. Using suitable methods, it helps them develop the same level of skills and abilities, so that later in primary school they find themselves at approximately the same level. We must always bear in mind that each child has its own personality and its own rate of growth.

Kindergarten teachers are provided with the opportunity to identify the personality traits of each child and to help it by creating opportunities that will contribute to its comprehensive development.

How We as Parents Help Our Children Enter the First School of Life: Kindergarten

We must emphasise that kindergarten plays an important role in preparing young children for primary school later. Therefore, the greater interest in and understanding of its importance we show as parents, the more we will help our child adapt to school life.

The first thing we must do as parents is to prepare ourselves for this transition so as to reduce our own anxiety and stress concerning future existent or non-existent problems that we may encounter in kindergarten. Children's antennas can detect any signal emitted by parents, whether verbal or not.

The more enthusiasm and optimism we show, the greater the sense of confidence we impart that everything will go well in the new school.

The child may ask questions such as, "Why do I have to go to a new school (if nursery school preceded) and lose my friends?"

It is advisable to use positive words when talking about kindergarten and to answer all questions truthfully so as not to create any doubt for the child about whatever he may want to learn. You can tell him that he is very lucky because he will make new friends and learn new things.

Generally speaking, preschool children do not face serious transition and adjustment problems in kindergarten. This is because they immediately enter a pleasant room full of toys, colourful drawings, chairs and tables their size; in other words, a warm and friendly environment.

Adjustment issues that parents may face at this age have more to do with:

- the level of autonomy the child has for simple every-day activities that up until then they relied on the parents for, such as: using the toilet on its own, wearing its shoes on its own, zipping up a jacket, buttoning its shirt and closing its bag. It is advisable for parents to use things or clothes that are child friendly and easy to use so as not to cause the child undue stress.

- the level of independence from family members, i.e. mother, grandmother, and father. Usually mothers, without realising it, become an obstacle to the child's smooth adjustment in kindergarten. When separated from their children, they feel a void that they try to fill by acting in ways that can make them feel useful and necessary, thus trying to maintain a dependent relationship with the child. That is how they transfer the psychological burden on the child, who has to face its own anxiety towards change.

There are mothers who come into the classroom with their children, helping them with their jackets and their bags, they take out their lunch boxes for them, all serving as a confirmation of their love when trying to say goodbye to their children.

They may however be really useful. How? By saying, for example, in a cheerful manner and with enthusiasm: "I am sure that today you will have a wonderful day with your teacher and your classmates!" Let's make sure that we do whatever we can to make going to school a cheerful and carefree activity.

It's a good idea to set a bedtime so that our children get enough sleep and become accustomed to waking up early as part of their daily routine.

It is a wonderful opportunity for children to visit the kindergarten with their parents on registration day. This will allow them to come into contact with the place, see how the children already attending spend their time there (if the school year has not ended yet), meet their teacher and get a taste of the new school. By the time the new school year commences, they will have had plenty of time to prepare themselves psychologically for the new situation.

What Does Kindergarten Offer Your Child?

During kindergarten, children learn how to behave and act in a group. They learn:

- to cooperate, to share things and ideas, to wait their turn, to speak politely, to obey rules, to take care of the environment

RULE

We never run in the classroom

- to be independent, to decide on their learning style and to experience the consequences of their decisions in a safe environment

- to learn the numbers and recognise what they mean

- to learn the letters and sounds and to begin recognising words as part of their lives

- to get to know books, to listen to stories or attempt to make up their own

- to improve their knowledge for several things and situations

- to develop the ability to use objects

- to understand through observation and try to explain a natural phenomenon

- to express feelings and exchange thoughts with each other

- to cultivate emotional intelligence, which involves learning how to handle their emotions by sharing experiences with other children

Characteristically, Robert Fulghum wrote in his book *All I Really Need To Know I Learned In Kindergarten*

> "*Wisdom was not at the top*
> *Of the graduate school mountain,*
> *But there in the sandpile at Sunday school.*
>
> *These are the things I learned:*
>
> *Share everything.*
> *Play fair.*
> *Don't hit people.*
> *Put things back where you found them.*
> *Clean up your own mess.*
> *Don't take things that aren't yours.*
> *Say you're sorry when you hurt somebody.*
> *Wash your hands before you eat.*
> *Take a nap every afternoon.*
>
> *Everything you need to know is in there somewhere.*
> *Take any of those items and extrapolate it into*
> *sophisticated adult terms and apply it to your*
> *family life or your work or your government or*
> *your world and it holds true and clear and firm.*
> *Think what a better world it would be.*"

How Is That Done? Through Play

Much research has been conducted on the importance of play, especially for preschool children. Through play, kindergarten tries to explore children's problems, needs and interests and to make good use of this innate desire children have in order to help them shape their personality.

Children have a vivid imagination and are intensely curious, they create theories about the world, are in constant contact with people and materials, investigate, constantly experiment with their natural surroundings and make symbolic representations, i.e. they pretend to take part in imaginary processes or pretend to be other people, animals and things when engaged in dramatic play. Through play, their linguistic capacity develops at a very fast pace and, given that their experiences proliferate rapidly, their interests extend to books and communication.

❧ ❧

The ability that children have to acquire such experiences through play, in combination with a suitable environment, has an impact on their neurological development. Children who are deprived of such experiences during their early years may have delayed brain development, which may later have a negative impact on learning. Research shows that during the early years of life a child has significant opportunities for normal neurological development.

Children of all ages love to play. On the other hand, since play has such an important role in a child's development, parents should show a particular interest in play and create the conditions that will allow and encourage children to express themselves through play.

DIFFERENT TYPES OF PLAY

Play – we repeat – is the most important activity for children because it contributes to their overall development, i.e. cognitive and language development, creativity, cooperation, social skills, and motor skills. When parents see their children playing, they should remember that they are practicing and cultivating the skills that will help them become good students later on in school.

Parents will better understand this when they see the skills they can develop through the following different kinds of play. They are:

1. *Physical play*, which involves moving various parts of the body, coordinating gross and fine motor skills i.e. activities involving arm and leg movements. These are a response to internal needs, but at the same time, basic psychomotor functions are put to use.

2. *Play with objects*, which involves toys that are a source of observation and interest, i.e. wind-up toys, toy cars, or materials used to construct things, which enables the child to use its imagination and creative abilities, i.e. clay, LEGO, etc.

3. *Role-playing games*. They can be fantasy or mimicking games. The child pretends to be a person, an animal, a tree and tries to find ways of expressing whatever he represents. In this manner, the child experiences situations that he would like to experience in everyday

life but is not given the opportunity to; thus, he sends messages to others who can comprehend the characteristics of his behaviour. If, for example, a preschooler pretending to be a father is very strict, it is quite likely that his own father displays similar behaviour.

4. *Team play or games with rules.* These games help the child function as a member of a team and become accustomed to obeying rules – either rules that the child itself made up or rules that were already set. Team play is the best means of socialisation for the child. When a child plays with other children or with adults, the social skills it acquires are invaluable. This type of play is a way for children to face their fears and their anxiety about things and situations in daily life that their parents and teachers are not always able to identify.

Combining these types of play is quite commonplace, i.e. role-playing can be done individually or in a group. When asked which of the above types of play are more effective for the development of a child, the answer is the one in which the child takes the initiative and decides on the rules to be obeyed, i.e. a self-guided game, as it uses all the skills acquired.

Spontaneous play in an environment focused on learning activities is the backbone of a successful educational programme in kindergarten. The kindergarten teacher has to create a stimulating environment and then should observe the children playing, interact with them, give them material, listen to their ideas and when necessary, guide them.

PARENTS, CHILDREN AND PLAY

Parents quickly discover that playing with their children is fun and useful. It is an easy and very effective way of learning about their children's interests, skills and concerns, as well as a way to show their own interest in and dedication to their children, and thus contribute to their development.

On a practical level, they can create opportunities for play by:

- inviting other children to the home

- visiting places where there are other children to play with

- taking children to places where they can meet people and see different things from what they see at home or at school

- adding imagination to everyday activities that children participate in

It is advisable for parents to avoid guiding their children's play. With their guidance, they deprive their children of the possibility to be creative and to find solutions to the problems presented; so children lose the opportunity to develop their confidence since their parents are presented as all-knowing in anything that may arise.

Parents should bear in mind that children's play depends on the needs, thoughts and sensitivities that children externalise at specific times, so the best games parents can offer them are those that stimulate their imagination and provide them with opportunities for creativity.

Children never stop asking for toys. Television constantly supplies children with ideas about what to ask for. Parents should be aware that when children ask for something it does not necessarily mean that they need it, nor that they may even want it. We should try to patiently explain to them that they will not be happier if we buy them all the toys they ask for because then toys lose their value and children lose their interest in them.

Play should remain memorable to children and parents can reminisce about happy moments they shared playing with their children in the past.

A useful tip would be to rotate various toys on a regular basis in order to rekindle a child's interest in an old toy and play with it again.

What's more, when we intend to visit a toy store, it's a good idea to have a discussion beforehand about what we are going to buy and we must keep this agreement. This way, it will be easier to control the situation and avoid constant pleading for more and more toys.

COOPERATION BETWEEN THE KINDERGARTEN AND THE FAMILY

Cooperation between the kindergarten and the family is invaluable for children's progress.

Good cooperation helps both children and their parents. When the children know that there is cooperation between their parents and the kindergarten teacher, they have an easier time adapting in the beginning and later become more responsive to instructions and regulations, both at school or at home.

This cooperation is beneficial to parents as it helps them to understand the importance of early childhood education and the need for their involvement in their children's education. They realise their role and responsibilities in the development of their children and helps them build a constructive relationship with the kindergarten teacher. The relationship is bidirectional because parents support the teachers' work when they speak to their children in a positive way about them and teachers receive the support and positive regard of parents through the feelings the children convey to them.

Kindergarten staff can advise parents on issues related to child-rearing in general, on how to monitor the development of the child at home, on extracurricular activities, on how to handle particular behavioural problems or issues concerning siblings who are primary school pupils or younger and not yet in school, etc.

The kindergarten teacher regularly schedules parent-teacher conferences in order to inform parents about their children's progress, as well as to give them the opportunity to visit the kindergarten at prear-ranged times and to ask various questions, such as:

- Does the child participate in group activities to a satisfac-tory degree?

- Does the child display difficulties being with other children?

- Has the teacher observed problematic behaviour that the parents should deal with?

- Can the teacher recommend other developmental activities to be done at home?

It is advisable for there to be a positive atmosphere during the con-ference with the kindergarten teacher. Cooperation can be considered successful when it is open and there is mutual trust and respect. This becomes apparent when, during the conference, parents show they trust the teacher's opinion and fully take into account any comments, suggestions or recommendations he/she may make.

Parents must bear in mind that educators are the people who moni-tor and observe their child throughout the school day and, as a result, are more objective. They can therefore, identify abnormal behaviour and inform parents about it. Even if parents are not satisfied with their discussion, they should not rush to draw conclusions and should try to be as objective as possible, however difficult it may seem.

They can cooperate to find solutions to problems and if they consid-er they need further assistance they can ask the kindergarten teacher for special help. In any case, they should have a positive attitude and not be biased nor become disappointed. Instead, they should consid-er any deviant behaviour as a motive for improvement and progress. Almost all things can be corrected as long as the people involved are committed to their goals, remain calm, and have patience and perseverance.

PARENTAL PARTICIPATION IN THE HYGIENE
OF KINDERGARTEN PUPILS

Parents should consult their paediatrician and the kindergarten teacher about issues concerning the care they should provide their children with in order to prevent or effectively deal with chronic illnesses, to help their children acquire healthy eating habits, to boost their immune system (i.e. vaccinations), and they should also attend kindergarten briefings in order to prevent environmental risks and accidents.

Controlling contagious diseases is a very serious problem and requires great responsibility on the part of the kindergarten and the parents. However, the main responsibility lies with parents because they are the first to observe changes in the behaviour and appearance of their child. It is advisable to keep a child at home once symptoms of an illness (virus, infection, cold, etc...) manifest themselves. Not keeping children at home when they are ill poses a great risk not only to their own health, but also to the health of their classmates. If the child has a contagious disease, then the parents should inform the kindergarten staff, even if the child remains at home.

HOW PARENTS CONTRIBUTE TO THE SMOOTH TRANSITION
OF THE CHILD INTO PRIMARY SCHOOL

Parents can significantly help their child better adapt to primary school by helping it develop basic communication and social skills, such as:

- being able to follow collective and individual instructions
- engaging in a guided activity after hearing all of the instructions

- completing a task it begins

- tidying up its things

- waiting its turn, as well as asserting itself

- listening to others attentively

- speaking clearly

- becoming self-sufficient and autonomous

- acquiring self-confidence

- showing self-control and handling conflicts without violence, for example, without pushing, punching, or biting

- behaving as a team member

- seeking help when needed

- identifying obvious dangers and avoiding them

- taking initiative

- understanding that losing is part of the game, just like winning is

- respecting the rules

- undertaking personal responsibility and teamwork

- making, justifying and implementing decisions

We can reasonably argue that all this cannot be accomplished from one day to the next. Of course, we will agree with you, though, if as parents you apply proper educational methods from the beginning, you will not have difficulty since these goals are fully aligned with the objectives of kindergarten school.

We should remember that within a relatively short period of time the child is called upon to gradually change the behaviour and habits it had in kindergarten and replace them with new behaviour, habits, and processes that are not only related to its development but to the learning process as well. How long it will take the child to balance and meet the new requirements depends on *how ready and able it is to cope with these changes.*

However, it is useful for the child to know that there will be some changes in its daily schedule so that it can respond to the school pro-gramme, which will include doing homework and preparing for the next day. We as parents need to remind our children that *these changes are tailor-made to their needs and they may apply them on their own* depending on the skills the child has developed until then.

CHAPTER 4

Primary School Begins

First Impressions

Starting primary school is a very important event both for the children themselves and also for their parents. Usually, when we first speak to the child about primary school, we tend to distinguish it from kindergarten by speaking in another tone or by expressing it in other words; for example, some parents refer to it as the "big school" in order to create the impression that it is important and more significant than kindergarten.

Therefore, by speaking to the child before school even starts, we help it form a first impression and prepare it psychologically for the big changes to come.

But how do we do this? What impression do we want to leave the child with after every discussion? How do we want the child to perceive school? As a burden, an encumbrance, something mandatory, stressful – a synonym for fear, terror, uncertainty, possibly punishment?

Or would we like it to feel as calm as possible, full of self-confidence and certainty; to see school as a challenge that provides new experiences and knowledge, a place that attracts and stimulates our interest; to be happy as it goes through the school door not only the first time – but for years to come?

❦   ❦

If that is what you really want, then you need to handle the issue as follows.

You must put emotional intelligence to use (as described above) and try to understand how your child feels about this change and what it would like to learn. It is preferable to listen to your child and discuss issues that concern him rather than bombard him with advice and information, some of which will be your response to questions, but most will burden him with extra weight and stress. It is like going to a doctor for some problem, and instead of asking you about your symptoms and the reason for your visit or examining you, he starts to give you medical advice, which will only cure your illness by pure coincidence.

How about trying to put ourselves in their place and thinking about how we would react to a significant change in our lives? A new job, a new residence for professional reasons, new duties, a promotion and so on.

In the beginning, everything seems very onerous because we are forced to change our habits, to become unsettled from the life style we are used to. The first thing we feel is shock and despair. Then comes denial; we do not want to believe it. Insecurity comes next, along with fear for upcoming changes. The excitement of novelty, the new prospects come into conflict with the fear that I might not make it in the new situation.

When we realise that there's no turning back, that change is a one-way road, then we enter the new phase of acceptance. It may take us a few hours to several years to arrive at this realisation. That's when we start to explore and ask about the event that marks a significant change in our life. Above all, we try to gather new information. Our behaviour depends on the type of information we receive and how we process it. Those who brought about the change – usually our supervisors – have an obligation to create the right atmosphere, to talk to us, answer our questions and to inform us about the benefits of this change. Then we gradually understand and enter the new reality more easily.

We adapt better to change and a new situation when other important factors and needs are respected and when the change provides some sort of satisfaction or benefit for us.

The child faces something similar when it first crosses the threshold of primary school: the child stands before a new reality, before the world of work, which requires organised and systematic effort, attention and concentration.

Taking all the above into consideration, our role is to help the child adapt as well as possible. How can this be achieved? By finding and implementing ways that will contribute to helping the child enter the new reality as smoothly as possible.

We must not forget that at this age children trust the only significant people in their life – that is, their mother and father – and less so the people in their close environment. It is therefore very important for parents to nurture and maintain this relationship of trust, which develops during this period.

It is true that children "listen" with their eyes and their ears. They carefully observe our body language and facial expressions to see if what we are telling them is true. That's why it is of essence that we ourselves truly believe what we tell our children, because, in this way, we will speak with certainty and confidence.

We have to decide on how to tell them whatever it is that we wish to tell them. We must speak calmly, in an encouraging and optimistic way, and with a smile. If we are calm, feeling no fear, insecurity and concern, and we keep an optimistic attitude, it is certain that we will convey these feelings to our children. As a result, our children feel safe and secure and are encouraged to use their strengths to face the new reality in the best possible way.

The basic phrase that should accompany any discussion with the child is: "I am certain that everything will be fine!" We say this phrase with a smile, self-confidence and the same certainty as telling somebody that the earth is round.

If you see that the child does not initiate any discussion, there are many opportunities you as a parent can take advantage of to start one such discussion. If we think about it, we get many chances on a daily basis to talk with our child and guide them as soon as they present them and we seize these opportunities.

For example, during the holidays when we are writing out our Christmas cards, we could ask our child, "Would you like to write Santa a letter and ask him for a gift?" We could take the opportunity to tell our child that Christmas time is approaching and that he will probably feel great satisfaction from doing so and how important it feels this action is.

During our daily visits to the supermarket when we approach the cashier to pay, we can say, "You know, Mary, checking the change we get after each payment is very important and it is something we all learn at your age. Do you understand how important that is?"

What we would consider a success would be to arouse enough

interest in the child so that it begins asking for what it wants to learn. And naturally, because the child sometimes asks the most improbable things, we should show gravity and interest in its queries and in no case should we disapprove of them and so decrease the value of what it has confided in us. If we do not face the child correctly, then the child will be afraid to confide in us in the future for fear that we might underestimate what is preoccupying it. Unfortunately, in this way, we prompt it to turn elsewhere, with unanticipated consequences and results.

What we should tell our child every day is that we will always love it and that we will always be available for anything it wants. That we are sure it will succeed, as it has done in the past, with other things it has learned to do. It is important to remind our child of the various small feats of the past, which seemed difficult then, but if it thinks about them now, they seem very easy. In this way, we stress the fact that they will not be asked to do the impossible, but something that we can guarantee they will be able to achieve. Anything that is taught in class is designed by people who know what a six-year-old child can do.

THE NEW PRIMARY SCHOOL PUPIL

We can see that the child is confronted with this new reality of school from the first day. Specific rules establish the child's relationship with the teacher and the other children, and define the structure of the lesson. Now the child has to consider all the "I musts" he is required to do from now on.

The new "I must dos" are designed by the state in order to organise learning at school in such a way as to have the optimal results for children. There is a detailed syllabus for each grade level of primary school as well as instructions on how to apply it, i.e. how to teach the subject matter and how to assess the teaching results. This detailed programme is designed in such a way as to correspond to the abilities of each age group. This means that children are capable of meeting the demands of organised learning, as long as we facilitate them by providing support, encouragement, time and confidence that they can do it.

The first days are usually a trial period and a time of concern for parents, who are waiting to see the feelings and reactions of their children. By the end of the first month, most children have usually adapted to this new reality and have overcome the anxiety and negative attitude of the first days of class.

FIRST CONTACT BETWEEN PARENTS AND SCHOOL

The primary school usually organises a first meeting with the parents of first-year pupils. Parents should attend this first parent-teacher conference because many useful issues concerning practical everyday matters are discussed, as are methods and behaviours parents should adopt in order to make the child's transition to primary school as smooth as possible. It is therefore very important to know what the school expects of our child and to be able to help it adapt and benefit to the fullest. These meetings are also the ideal place to express our questions or concerns.

What the school asks of us is to offer it our support as parents. What this means is that we should participate and help the school in its effort to provide a comprehensive, harmonious and balanced structure and environment in which pupils can develop their cognitive and intellectual abilities. We accept and respect its rules.

Cooperation, the Magic Word

Parents know the personality and behaviour of their child at home while teachers know its learning abilities and behaviour at school. Co-operation between the two – parents and teachers – is a prerequisite and guarantee for the child's proper development.

It is not possible for a child to succeed when the people he considers important in his life, namely his parents and his teachers, are on opposing sides. It will be difficult to both shape its behaviour and organise its work.

Parents and teachers should share information about the child, ask for suggestions for progress, discuss the difficulties that might exist and agree on what both sides can do to have the best results for the child.

This effort must last throughout primary school as it increases its expectations from one grade to the next and the child is required to adjust well to the new conditions each time.

Teachers, on the other hand, can provide parents with invaluable guidance not only because they have completed specialised studies in the field but also because they have taught a great number and wide range of pupils and are probably more experienced in the matter.

- They inform parents about the multifunctional role the school plays and urge them not to focus only on its academic role. For example, they stress the importance of cooperation and the socialisation of children through various events and volunteer activities

- They inform parents not only about their child's academic performance but also about their general behaviour at school

- They try to discretely obtain information on the family situation and the people who may exert influence on the pupil

- They recommend and encourage meetings with specialists (i.e. psychologist, family counsellor or special therapist) if they detect deviant behaviour, learning difficulties, dyslexia, autism, etc.

- They encourage creative leisure activities that help

release pent-up energy and are channels of emotional expression

- They point out the negative consequences of excessive television viewing and computer use at home

- They stress the importance of setting and respecting limits both at home and at school

For all these reasons, we should trust teachers not only for the information they provide concerning our child, but for any other queries and concerns that may arise along the way.

We may make surprising discoveries as to the character of our children because many times others "see" things in our children that we don't. This will help us gain a broader perspective on our child and we may realise that our children have special characteristics and display behaviours that are not evident on a daily basis. By this we mean behaviour that is not displayed in the family environment and which can be either positive or negative.

How to Convey Positive Messages about the Importance of School to Our Children

Many times, without realising it, we complicate or facilitate our children's adjustment at school in various ways. So, we "convey" messages not only to our children but also to the teachers about how important we think school is. Over time, our attitude is conveyed to our children, and that's why we have to be very careful.

If the child arrives late to class or as soon as the lesson begins, he has started off his day on the wrong foot. He has missed the chance to adapt to the school environment and possibly an announcement made by the headmaster/mistress about some school matter, such as an excursion or a change in the next day's programme. The child has surely missed the opportunity for a little chat or a little game time with friends before the lessons begin. Besides this, the child feels bad in front of their teacher and fellow pupils when it repeatedly arrives late for school because it needs the acceptance of the teacher and its classmates.

A child has no sense of time; we must be the ones to organise its schedule and make sure it has enough time to prepare for school and not be late. If we delay the child's arrival at school, we convey the message that school is not so important, because when we're interested in where we're going and care about our obligations, we're on time.

The same message is conveyed when the teacher asks the children to bring something from home for class or an event, i.e. a piece of cardboard, materials for Easter crafts, or other events, and our children go to school empty-handed.

We must note that the absence from various school events, such as carnival events, trips, or visits to the theatre or to a museum without any valid reason deprives the child of experiences as important as any lesson.

The child loses the opportunity to:

1. develop closer relationships with peers,

2. learn by observation

The next day the child may feel isolated from the other children and the teacher who participated in the event and are exchanging impressions and experiences of the shared activity.

If there is a health problem, financial or family difficulties that prevent a child from taking part in various activities, the parents must first of all respect the child and discuss what is happening with his teachers so as to ensure the acceptance and love that the child may be trying to get from its classmates.

If we wish our child to succeed in this new world of school, all the rules and obligations should acquire the importance and seriousness bestowed upon them by the school itself, regardless of what they may mean to us as adults in our daily lives.

Whatever our child hears from its teachers is very important for it and it wants to repeat it continuously. We may not totally agree with what we hear, but it is of vital importance for the child. It is an indication that the child has satisfactorily adjusted to the school environment. The child has accepted its role as a student and is trying to fulfil its new tasks.

If, however, we do not agree with the teacher's opinion or with the teaching methods used, we should in no way undermine the teacher's personality in front of the child because in so doing we automatically discredit the role of the teacher and her influence on our child. It is preferable to arrange a meeting to exchange views and get answers to our questions that concern us rather than tear down the child's hero, whom we will need later for another matter that will occupy us in the future.

What Is Learning and How Is it Done?

Learning is the acquisition of knowledge, experience, skills; skills through which a change in the individual's behaviour occurs. It is a process through which we form ourselves and which lasts our entire life and allows us to see, to choose, to believe, to act, to think and to behave differently from before.

Learning is done in many ways and is differentiated according to the different age groups. In the early years of our life, we learn by observing, monitoring, mimicking, receiving guidance and testing. The knowledge a preschool child acquires is diverse and concerns skills. For example, it learns to talk, to walk, to sit, to get dressed, to eat using cutlery, to wash itself, to tie its shoelaces, to assemble puzzles, to recognise different types of music, to speak a foreign language, to behave, to say please and thank you, and much more.

But when school starts, learning is undertaken in a methodical and organised way; this does not mean, however, that the child doesn't continue to learn through observation.

In school, learning is acquired after proper planning and preparation, with the teacher's guidance, with the appropriate educational material, and with the cooperation and communication of all those involved in this process. The role of the school is to ensure that children of the same age are taught the same things. In other words, children the same age develop together and simultaneously advance to the next level.

How effective school learning is depends on various factors that will be analysed in later chapters. It basically depends on the readiness of pupils to learn and how prepared they are to adapt to the school programme and to successfully advance through all the stages of learning in primary school.

Why Does a Child Learn?

A child learns when it is able to cover one of its needs by acquiring a new skill or knowledge. For example, a child learns to tie its shoelaces when neither of its parents is around to help, or it tries to learn how to swim because it feels it is lacking in this skill and expects to derive pleasure from it.

Children learn things that are related to their interests more quickly and easily. A young boy may learn the names of all the players of a football team with impressive speed, but cannot learn history. The reason is very simple. As a football player himself, the young boy is interested in football, while he is not interested in history. If he is a member of a football team, then he trains to become a better football player. Another child learns to use the computer keyboard when trying to play a game. Children pick up a foreign language when a television show or movie they are watching is not dubbed.

In order for children to want to learn, they need incentives, which can vary from child to child, depending on their behaviour. We as parents should carefully observe the reactions and attitudes of our children toward the learning process.

We may observe that our children show no desire to learn what we or the school wish them to. This does not always mean that they are unable or do not have the skills to do so. They may feel that they do not need this particular type of knowledge or they may not understand why they have to learn the specific subject or they may find it terribly boring to sit and study for an hour or two. It could be that the school or home environment cause feelings of anxiety in the child, or that we, the parents, are putting too much pressure on them to perform better.

Therefore, it is very important to observe the psychological state of our children and to try to understand their inner world so that we could help them develop their own incentives.

Children sometimes ask us things that we do not expect for their age, such as why we cannot see in the dark and how far the sun is from earth. A child that expresses such queries has its own internal motives to listen to the schoolteacher and it learns during the delivery of the lesson, in the deepest meaning of the term. It is very likely that he will not need to study much at home but rather he will seek some other book to read, he will ask questions, he will have the thirst to learn something new. This child may be bored with the daily tasks and may not want to do the homework, *yet he has real motives to learn.* This child can function marvellously in the school system but without experiencing the pressure of studying in order to get good marks.

All children need to have their own motives, which don't necessarily have to be the same as ours but can prove effective and lead to success in school.

WHAT MAKES LEARNING DIFFICULT?

What factors hinder the desire and willingness to learn? Which of these factors can parents address using the appropriate interventions?

Children have difficulty learning in the following cases:

- When they do not understand why they have to learn

- When they cannot relate what they're learning with themselves, their interests, their plans, and in general, with whatever concerns them

- When the learning environment threatens their personality without providing any encouragement

We must understand that the learning process is like an exploratory mission during which a person is constantly tried and tested; one often succeeds but also runs the risk of facing disapproval when one doesn't. Even though conditions may not always be encouraging, children often have to try again and again until they succeed.

Parents often ask children for proof that they have learned something. We would better understand our children if we put ourselves in their place. Let's imagine ourselves being asked to learn something whose purpose we don't understand and that we cannot relate to. Imagine what it feels like to be assessed and judged by someone authorised to see if we have learned something well. Imagine feeling that our acceptance by the people we need and love depends on our performance in this process.

If we could put ourselves through this ordeal, which the adult world calls "a carefree childhood", we would understand how much help and encouragement our children need in order to be willing and able to learn what the educational system is offering them.

❀   ❀

Combining Obligations and Needs

What can a child expect when returning home from school?

Usually it expects to be allowed to do spontaneous things like playing or relaxing, thus relieving the stress and fatigue of the day. At least that's what the child used to do in the past when it returned home from preschool or kindergarten.

When a child goes to primary school, it sees the school somehow invading its home life by dictating rules and tasks and assigning work and study at home. So it wonders when it will be allowed to do something that it wants and loves, something that has been postponed for so many hours because of school attendance and study.

Therefore, in order to make it easier for our child to come to terms with the reality of a pupil's life and to be able to adjust to the demands of school, we need to help it organise its study time so that it has enough free time to relax and do whatever it likes. Mostly, this new situation must respect the child's other needs, such as its need for play, which we mentioned above, and other activities.

If we apply this tactic, we will see that our child will not resent the time it has to devote to schoolwork.

A Pupil's Job Is Tough...

It is very important to emphasise here that every person who has to learn new things on a daily basis has specific time and quantitative limits, along with a precise speed at which he can absorb new knowledge.

If we surpass our limits, our mental abilities abandon us, our cognitive processes become blocked, and eventually, the learning process comes to a halt. The fact that we learn different things every day does not necessarily mean that we have time to assimilate them and to put them into practice.

At work, we adults apply techniques and knowledge that we have already acquired. We improve our knowledge along the way by attending seminars and training programmes, but this is not done on a daily basis. In this way, we make our work easier and expend less effort because we have access to knowledge we have acquired in the past as well as to new knowledge we acquire in the present.

A schoolchild does not have this luxury. The pupil's job is very difficult and tedious because it has to learn something completely new every day. Imagine a doctor having to deal with a new disease every day, or an employee having to use a different procedure on a daily basis.

Organising Study Time at Home

According to the educational system of some developed countries, the study and preparation for the next day is done at school during the school lessons in collaboration with the teacher. However, in most countries, education is so structured that study and preparation for the next day is done at home. When this is the case, the child's study time should take precedence on the family schedule over any other obligation, and only as an exception and after discussion should homework be left for later.

We parents should take every opportunity to convey the message that schoolwork and homework, which is preparation for school, is very important.

Where a child does its homework and studies is directly related to the child's performance. It is important to remember that each part of the house has its own use. So, it is not a good idea for children to do their homework in the kitchen or in the living room or on the floor. The child's room is the ideal place for study because it is protected from other stimuli that can distract the pupil, plus, this cultivates the belief that the study area should be one's personal space, which at the same time offers a sense of security to the child.

The desk should be used exclusively for studying and for no other purposes, i.e. dining or games. The desk should be tidy and should have all the necessary writing material (i.e. notebooks, pencils, erasers, books, etc.) at hand. There should be no unnecessary objects such as markers, story books, and toys on the surface.

Now that we have found the proper study area, we will turn to the organisation of the child's schoolbag. It's something we must pay attention to. The more organised a child's things are, the better and more organised its studying will be. Every time the child starts to study, he should empty out his bag and pack the books he will need for next day.

The school schedule should be posted somewhere where it is visible to the child (i.e. over the desk). The child identifies the correct day (time orientation) and finds the books, notebooks and whatever else he needs for the next day's classes.

Then the child should put them in the order he wishes to study them, which may be according to the degree of difficulty, the volume, or preference of the subjects he wants to start with. There are subjects that the child can work on alone, such as copying, spelling, basic arithmetic, reading, etc. These are usually considered "easy" by the child while all the other tasks are considered "difficult". At this point, we make it clear to the child that these two words do not exist. All subjects are the same. We realise of course that the child will need more help in some subjects and less in others. Children feel greater security when they understand that their parents will help them with some difficult subjects if needed and that they are always there for them.

In the beginning, we work with the children and show them the whole procedure. It's not a bad idea to make a small table, like the one below, showing the tasks to be completed, and putting a check mark upon completion *with the child*. The check mark system should be used until the child has understood the procedure and has established a study routine.

Preparing for studying

✓   I go to the toilet and then drink water

✓   I empty my bag

✓   I look at the school schedule

✓   I find the books I need

✓   I arrange what I do not need in my bookcase
    and place anything that has been corrected in the
    right folder.

✓   I place the books and notebooks in the order I
    want to study

✓   I check which tasks I have to complete

We should designate a specific study time dedicated to homework. This time will not be the same for all children; each child has its own pace and speed at which it is able to work.

At this point, it is useful to consult our child's teachers because they are the specialists that can suggest the best methods we should apply and the time we should allocate for our child's study time. Of course, the method applied at home should be closely related to the method applied in school. The teacher knows the pace at which our child works and can show us ways to make study at home effective. Experts say that for the most fruitful results, pupils in the first three years of primary school should devote 20 to 30 minutes to study, while those in the 4th, 5th, and 6th year should devote 30-45 minutes. After this time period, a child's performance begins to decline.

It is essential for the child to feel our presence next to it at the beginning of its school life. Gradually, though, we should start to distance ourselves, first from the preparation phase of studying (table 1) – we allow it two minutes to arrange books – and then from the studying itself – we allow it to work on its own for four minutes, and so on. The goal is for the child to be able to do more of its homework and studying alone as it progresses from one grade level to the next. If we do not implement this at the beginning, then we convey the wrong message; namely, that studying involves both of us (i.e. both the child and the mother or father). If this is not done, the child will not realise that studying concerns him alone.

❧   ❧

After the child has completed its homework, it is important to discuss what the child found difficult and what it thought of the whole process. If we are pleased with the result, we reward it with phrases such as, "I am proud of how you worked today. I think it went very well, you were calm and you concentrated. What do you think?"

If on the contrary things did not go well, you can say, "I saw that you had a hard time today. But I'm sure tomorrow you will do really well, you will try to work more calmly. Just ask me if there's anything you don't understand and I am sure you will do very well. How do you feel? What do you think went wrong? Why? What will you do differently tomorrow?"

When we see that the child has made a few mistakes, we draw the child's attention to them. At first we say, 'There's a mistake in this word/ equation' and afterwards, 'in this sentence/exercise' and urge the child to self-correct its work. If the child cannot identify the mistake, we first explain the point, and then encourage it to identify and correct the mistake. If it still fails to find the mistake, then we correct it together.

If the child has poor handwriting – in copying exercises – we try to encourage the child to produce better handwriting by saying, "Do you think this is your best handwriting? I'm sure you can write better. Do you want to try?" It is important to identify mistakes at the beginning of the writing exercise, so that the child won't have to erase and re-write the whole text, which would greatly displease any child.

When and Under What Conditions Should Study Take Place?

Homework should be done at a time when the child is best able to concentrate and perform.

Some children perform better after taking a nap at noon, others after relaxing with a favourite pastime and others prefer to do their homework immediately after lunch.

It makes sense to experiment in the beginning until we discover what the best schedule for our child is. We will quickly discover when studying is more fruitful and *determine when studying should start and end*.

The next step is to determine the amount of time to be spent on studying and to schedule the breaks the child will have, taking into consideration what the teacher has recommended as well as our child's speed and pace. It is very important that the child know that the time designated for homework is predetermined so that it will not rush to finish and do sloppy work in order to go and play. At the same time, the child will gradually learn to manage his study time so as to make good use of the time he has at his disposal.

Our attitude towards our children's school obligations should be positive and we should convey the message that study time is an activity that is interesting, useful and constructive and which we enjoy engaging in with our child. In so doing, we will help our child acquire a positive attitude towards study and homework. We can help our child organise its time as well as possible and should be available in case it needs guidance. We can *share the work with our children*, not do the homework for them, and in this way establish a channel of communication with our child and share a common interest.

It is not wise to extend the time set for homework because if we surpass the limits, the child basically stops performing. Furthermore, if despite your efforts to make the best use of substantial study, you see that the child procrastinates and is distracted by other things, do not extend homework time by more than 5-10 minutes. After that, you must allow the child to go to school without having completed its homework so that it can face the consequences of its actions, which showed a lack of discipline. Teachers can provide support to the efforts parents make if they have kept close contact and have open channels of communication.

The quality and duration of study time is influenced not only by how happy the child is to do its homework but also by the conditions under which study time takes place. A child will not be able to study when there is yelling, crying, and fussing beforehand or if studying is viewed as a punishment for the child.

Also, we should make sure to designate a particular place of study for the child where it can concentrate and not be distracted by other stimuli such as noise, conversation, television, music or visitors.

What's particularly important, at least in the beginning when the child is young and before it has reached the stage where it can responsibly meet the school's demands on its own, is to not make the child feel that it is missing out on really pleasant things when it is doing its homework. It is not pleasant for the pupil to hear its mother playing with its younger sister, or the rest of the family talking, laughing or watching television. So, for this reason, TURN THE TV OFF, TURN THE TV OFF!

It would be best if, during this time, the rest of the family also engage in some activity that requires concentration, like reading or writing, or at least some activity that can be done quietly. It is the best example we can give our child in order for it to understand that everyone needs to seriously occupy themselves with work done at home.

If there are younger siblings in the family, they should be doing something else outside the home or engaging in another activity when the child is studying.

If there are two schoolchildren in the family that have to do homework, make sure their study time coincides, so as not to have one child engaged in something "pleasant" while the other is doing something "disagreeable" or rather, a "demanding" activity. It is not easy to concentrate when your dad or your siblings are enjoying a game on the play station!

We should stress the importance of quiet time to our children and urge them to organise their study time properly so that when one child is studying a demanding lesson for which it will probably need our help or guidance, the other is doing something it can work on without our help. For example, if a child is learning spelling, the other one can be doing exercises, and when the first is ready for a spelling check, the other one can study history, and so on. In this way, an effective cooperative attitude will be established and adopted during study time.

What's more, children really enjoy talking and cooperating with each other and their parents. With the above-mentioned study method, *peer-teaching* is promoted and serves as an alternative to parental assistance. In other words, the older child may take a break, after having done their easy exercises, and help the younger child. So, on the one hand, he consolidates his knowledge and on the other, he learns to behave calmly and respectfully, putting himself in his sibling's shoes.

There may be tension, but parents should use this opportunity in such a way as to teach their children to resolve conflicts quickly and peacefully.

It is advisable to wait for the children to finish their homework so that family members can do things they enjoy together, even if it means watching their favourite television programme later.

The message that is conveyed is that the parents recognise that what the children are doing is very important and are reflecting it with their behaviour.

Another factor we shouldn't forget is that every change, like the one we mentioned above; namely, the child's induction into primary school and new obligations for young students, must respect the life-style and needs the child had prior to this change if we wish to maintain a healthy balance between its personal and school life.

How can we do this?

a. By ensuring free time for the child. First of all, we must attend to and carefully plan our child's free time. A child should have free time. Real free time. We should not fill every afternoon with extracurricular activities, like swimming, music, sports, dance, painting, foreign languages, etc. Let us choose the activities our child will engage in wisely and according to the needs of the child.

A child needs to have a creative and relaxing time for school obligations and free time to meet new people and socialise with peers without a specific schedule. Children are more carefree when their day is planned and organised, when study time and leisure time have been planned.

b. Allowing time to adjust to the new way of life. We should not expect our child or ourselves to get the hang of things right away.

How Can we Facilitate Study Time for the Child?

There are several suggestions on how best to assist our child with its daily homework.

- We should encourage our child to manage its time properly in order for it to use its time effectively and not stray from the study programme. The child will not immediately acquire the skill of organising its time – that is the only certainty – but it will have started processing the whole procedure and will, at some point, master it.

- We mustn't forget that proper time management is something we strive to achieve throughout our entire personal and professional life. How beneficial it would have been if we had managed to organise ourselves a few decades ago!

- We should be available to answer any questions or give our opinion on something that we know.

- We must remember that it is not important that our child learn a lesson by heart, or copy something from another source for a project, or prepare for the next day's lesson. The only purpose for all of the above is to convince the teacher that the child studies a lot at home. What *is* important is to help the child learn what he is trying to learn at school and much more not only for the next day, but for its whole life.

- We should speak to the child at every opportunity – or better still, we should create opportunities for discussion. We can comment on something that has made an impression on us or that we saw in the street and ask for the child's opinion.

- Whatever we say should be worded properly; we should be clear and specific.

- We should often ask "why", and tell our child we did not understand something and ask it to explain it to us if it has better understood.

- We should talk to our child about a book we have read and really liked

- We can discuss something he read and liked in one of his schoolbooks and comment on it.

- We should talk about the things that interest it, i.e. basketball, football, another team sport that the child may not even know, but may be interested in. We ask the child to tell us what it really likes about this game and actively listen while it is explaining and commenting on it.

- We should practise active listening. We listen carefully to the child each time it speaks so as to understand what it is trying to say, how it feels about something that happened at school, what it's concerned about and what it expects of us.

For example, the child comes home from school and says, "My teacher doesn't like me." At that moment, we should ask, "Why do you say that?" First of all, we show that we are carefully listening to what our child is saying and are waiting for it to explain how it is feeling. We give it the opportunity to talk about it. The child explains what happened and what made it come to that conclusion. We ask it how it feels about what happened, and how in its opinion things could have been done better. By speaking about the matter, the child has the opportunity to justify why it happened so that it can understand how its relationship with that particular teacher and subject works.

If we react negatively and say things like: "Maybe the teacher called on you and you didn't know the answer", "Your teacher does not have issues with other students, so maybe you did something?" or "Well, tomorrow I'll come to school and talk to her" directly condemns the child without hearing what he has to say and without actually communicating with him. We have answered according to what we had in mind. We should avoid doing so.

At other times, our child comes home and announces something it heard or learned at school, or something that happened to a friend during the break. Whatever we are occupied with at that moment, it is best to sit down and listen to the child, and ask for clarification if necessary, offering our opinion, if it is relevant to what the child is saying.

If, for example, the teacher talked about racism, we can develop the child's humanitarian feelings by discussing how many children are saved daily in Africa because of contributions made by UNICEF and other organisations. In so doing, we involve the child in a discussion from which he learns much more than he would have learned by trying to understand the lesson.

What is important is that children cannot have such discussions at school, at least not to the extent we can at home, because their schedule at school is tightly packed and there are time limits on such activities.

What we manage to do is fill in the missing pieces of information as we would the missing pieces of a puzzle, which, when completed and all the pieces fit together, acquires its true meaning, and all the pieces together make up a whole. This is in fact what learning is all about.

When, for example, our child does not understand something in science class, we can draw examples from everyday phenomena or initiate conversations that are unrelated with schoolwork in order to arouse its interest and help it learn.

Another factor related to this process is the incentives and motivation we inspire in our children to help them develop their creative thinking.

For example, we can ask the child, "What would happen if the earth were three times bigger than what it is, what effect would this change have on people's lives?" "What would happen if we did not feel heat on our planet?" "How else could we use a pencil case?" "How many different ways are there to have a treasure hunt?"

We can see if and how creative our children are from the number of ideas they have as well as from how innovative they are.

How Can We Tell If Our Child Is Creatively Gifted?

a. If it is sensitive to environmental problems. Such a child is more sensitive and better understands the environmental impact than other children.

b. If we observe an optimistic attitude which manifests itself with questions like, "How would you do this?" rather than "Is that possible?"

c. If we distinguish spontaneous enthusiasm rather than doubt about whether something can actually be put into practice. The doubt would actually hinder rather than promote creativity.

d. If it can 'think outside the box', approach and solve a problem in innovative ways or think of different uses for an everyday object, apart from its common use.

e. If its thoughts and judgments do not depend on the praise or disapproval of others, but are based on its own assessments.

The talented and creative student usually has the following characteristics: He shows intense curiosity about the things around him, asks many and varied questions and queries, is sensitive to what is going on around him, and can visualise things and actions from their descriptions. He has the rare gift of understanding the processes of problem solving, which he can express in a variety of ways, such as through painting, prose, music, poetry, drama and he can even find solutions for common problems. He develops and constructs new mechanical means, easily adapts to new situations which he enjoys, often comes into conflict with and questions the generally accepted status quo; his actions may be unexpected, he can easily generalise what he has learned and apply it to completely different situations. (Paraskevopoulos, 1985, 3rd Volume).

It is, however, very important that from the moment we see such traits in the child, to discuss them with the teacher, although it is likely that it will not exhibit the same curiosity and appreciation for school work. The teacher, within the framework of cooperation we have fostered, can advise us on how to guide this artistic child's spiritual skills in the right direction.

Mostly children in the 1st, 2nd and 3rd years of primary school display such heightened originality in their ideas and actions, while in the 4th year there is a downturn in this phenomenon. This is mainly due to the fact that, at the age of 9, the child complies with the internal rules and stereotypical behaviour patterns applied by the school, which do not encourage creative thinking.

According to I. Paraskevopoulos, Professor of General Psychology, the personal and social obstacles to the development of creative thinking are the following:

- A lack of love and of a sense of psychic security

- Authoritarian behaviour and a lack of freedom

- The anxiety of making a mistake

- Constant criticism

- Rigid adherence to widely accepted rules and regulations

- Excessive emphasis on competition or cooperation

- Lack of confidence in ourselves and in our creative abilities

- Absolute trust in logic

- The pursuit of perfection

- A blind acceptance of the infallibility of our superiors

- Our reluctance to insist on a great number of solutions to a problem

- A negative and indifferent attitude in dealing with various problems around us

- The pursuit of safety and certainty

- The fear of appearing foolish or ridiculous

THE DEVELOPMENT OF MEMORY

Our memory is a repository of all our experiences that the brain retains for future use for a short or long period of time after their acquisition. It is a key factor in learning throughout all levels of primary school and the application of various mnemonic techniques facilitates its ability to retain information.

Memory is divided into three stages:

a. Encoding. It is the first information processing step in which the sensory stimuli are converted into mental representations, in accordance to various mnemonic codes (Vosniadou 2001), in order to allow their input and processing in the memory system.

b. Storage. It is the stage where information, which has been processed and encoded, is stored in long-term memory for long periods.

c. Retrieval. Retrieval is the stage during which the information stored in memory is detected and restored on a conscious level. The process of information retrieval varies in the mechanisms used and the ease and accuracy of restoration and depends on how information was encoded in memory.

Memory is distinguished according to the length of retention into the sensory, the short-term and long-term memory.

a. *The sensory memory*. Lasts from roughly 1/10 second to 4 seconds. It is the memory that retains the incoming sensory stimuli as long as it needs in order that the brain be given the essential time to compare it with stored information, to recognise it and to choose the elements that will become objects of further processing. It concerns the images (audio or visual) that are the first perceptual depictions of exterior stimuli. They are recorded as they are without any processing.

b. *The short-term memory.* It is the storage space where the images are immediately transferred after their passage from the sensory organs.

1. The information it contains lasts from 15 to 20 seconds unless the individual intervenes with various mnemonic techniques, such as focusing his attention on it, and retains it for longer (theoretically indefinitely). Or otherwise, one can achieve this with internal repetition. For example, we remember a telephone number if we repeat it enough times.

2. The amount of information that can fit the short-term memory simultaneously is limited. Research suggests (George Miller, American psychologist) that the adult can retain 7 +/- 2 units of information simultaneously. Each additional new unit of information displaces an older piece of information and takes its place. One way to increase the capacity of short-term memory is to organise information into subgroups with comprehensive content. For example, a complicated number such as 2433253 can be retained as $24=2\times12$ months, the 33 years of Christ and 253 for 25th March.

c. *The long-term memory.* It is the space in which the vast amount of information that we have acquired in the course of our life is stored. This information was in the short-term memory and it underwent the process of *mnemonic consolidation* (activity of coding, internal repetition). Thus, it became permanent information in the long-term memory. The capacity of long-term memory is theoretically unlimited.

From the long-term memory, information can be retracted to the short-term memory if it does not exist there the moment the short-term memory needs this information.

Of all the phases of the memory processes, the short-term memory is the only conscious cognitive function. Only in this memory space, can the individual act upon and apply the various forms of memori-sation. Also, only in this space can the individual be informed of both the more recent and older information that has been stored. (Paraskev-opoulos, 1985, 3rd volume)

This analysis is useful in order for us to better understand at what age the child can use the various mnemonic techniques, i.e. internal repetition and organisation of the material in comprehensive categories to facilitate school learning.

It has been noted that from the age of six, there is an increase in the use of internal repetition as an effective mnemonic technique. Many children do not discover this technique on their own, but use it if suggested by someone else. Therefore, the parent should suggest that a first-year child repeat a new letter or syllable to be learned many times. To a certain extent, the same procedure should be followed in the higher levels respectively.

It has been observed that children from 6-10 years of age use repe-tition mechanically, i.e. they repeat things one by one; while children aged 10 years and over use repetition after they have organised infor-mation in such a way as to facilitate the procedure. For example, they put titles and names on objects they must learn. (Paraskevopoulos, 1985, 3rd Volume).

It is helpful for parents to know that the factors that influence memory are related to the individual as well as to the material to be memorised. In other words, the same individual does not memorise all types of information with the same ease all hours of the day. For example, a child who is the visual type should be shown material it is being taught visually and repeatedly so that the image is strong when the information is transferred to the long-term memory.

Above all, we must be aware that the mnemonic ability is a dynamic process (Piaget) which is gradually acquired as the child goes from one developmental period to the next and therefore it is inherent in the course of cognitive development.

Research has shown that children aged nine (in the 4th year of primary school) and over are able to choose the strategy that makes it easier for them to learn something. So until the age of nine, the parent must suggest the appropriate procedures and the necessary techniques for the best possible results, with the teacher's advice, of course, because they know our child and can monitor its progress.

GRADING AND ASSESSMENT IN PRIMARY SCHOOL

Right before the Christmas holidays – depending always on each school's programme – many families go through a period of anxiety or, at best, anticipation for the school grades.

After third year, children and parents alike impatiently wait to see what grades the children will bring home, what they are 'worth', how good they are as students and, by extension, how worthy and competent *their parents* are. These views may sound a bit over the top to some of our readers but still, it is a reality that expresses an unfortunately large portion of the educational community.

The main objective of the assessment process in primary schools nowadays is to give feedback on the educational process and to identify difficulties so as to improve the education offered to the pupil and to help the pupil make progress.

Assessment is deemed necessary in education, as in any other goal-oriented and structured procedure that requires planning, achieving goals, applying strategy and, finally, evaluating the work undertaken. Apart from this necessity though, there is also the educational purpose of assessment, because, to put it simply, it gives feedback to both teachers and students concerning the effectiveness of their activities. In other words, it defines the response patterns of both students and teachers during the educational process, using reward and rejection.

So, what can we do as parents so that the mandatory grading process can help and advance the cognitive as well as psychosocial development of our child?

It is crucial to explain to the child that a number (for example 8 or 9) or a letter (for example B or C) cannot contain the extent of one's personality and thus, it doesn't carry the same weight as a detailed evaluation, which may refer to specific parts of a lesson. For example, a child may experience difficulties in spelling during the language lesson. This does not mean that our child is a 'bad' student when it comes to language in general. What we should do is explain to the child that a low grade does not mean that it is incompetent but that it needs to try harder in order to understand the more demanding parts better and cover specific cognitive gaps of the specific subject.

We ought to avoid comparing our child to its classmates and, more importantly, we should not make it feel that the grades are of great importance to us. Frequently, knowingly or unknowingly, we make our child feel tremendously pressured and we compel it to 'chase' after good grades so that we do not feel inferior in our social milieu (between friends, family) or so that the child can acquire a desired object or even our acceptance and love.

Of course, we should not undermine the importance of assessment. On the contrary, the grades should constitute a reason for discussion with the young student so that we can reinforce the importance of constant effort and self-improvement. This is achieved if we identify and stress the possible strengths of the child and based on these, urge him to improve on his weaker points.

At the same time, by discussing the causes of a low grade and ways of dealing with it, on one hand, we build a relationship based on trust and acceptance between our child and us; on the other hand, we provide it with a highly valuable lesson on self-awareness and ways of overcoming difficulties. In the opposite case – good grades – we make an example of rewarding those who deserve it after a great success. However, the most important thing is that our child begins to learn to accept success as much as failure and to persevere on its path with its parents as allies, regardless of its grades.

Children mostly receive the non-verbal messages we convey while learning in various ways but also by imitating behaviours and values of the important people that surround them (Bandura's Social Learning Theory).

So then, we, as parents and teachers, ought to develop so that our children can do the same.

Finally, even if we disagree with the teacher, for the sake of our child, we should not discredit them in their presence, directly or indirectly, because then we deprive our child of even the slightest gain from the educational procedure. We should let the children judge for themselves and listen to their reasoning, but we should avoid taking a stance. State your disagreement by providing facts if you are asked to, but go no further. Of course, the teachers should do the same. The people who are significant in a child's life ought to – if nothing else – be treated with the proper attention and respect. (Matsagouras, 2008a; Kapsalis, 1998)

PARENT-TEACHER RELATIONSHIPS

The parent-teacher relationship should be based on honesty and cooperation. It is not a difficult goal to achieve as long as certain practical guidelines are followed.

1. We should believe that the school wants communication and cooperation with us.

2. We should not hesitate to ask for clear information on whatever concerns we may have about the schoolwork. We should, for example, ask the teacher what material will be covered by the end of the year and what the child will have learned.

3. We should try to understand what is expected of us when the teacher asks us to do some things. For example, we could ask for clarifications regarding homework, what our contribution should be and to what extent? We should ask for details.

4. We should not be afraid to express to the teacher what our intentions are, what we are willing and what we are not willing to do and to explain why.

5. We should express our opinion and our objections to an assessment made by the teacher or on some values promoted by the school

6. We should discuss our child's study habits at home and ask for ideas and suggestions in order to have better results.

CHAPTER 5

The Psychosocial Development of Preschool and School-Age Children

DURING OUR CHILDREN'S TIME IN KINDERGARTEN and in primary school, we the parents realise that their habits, their behaviour and their preferences change. The basic reason is that during school age, children undergo important changes in their psychosocial development. The child leaves the narrow environment of the family and enters the world of organised work. For many years, it will attend this institution and will cooperate with 20-25 children under the guidance and the supervision of a schoolteacher.

The child now has two roles to play: the role of the pupil and the role of the classmate.

As a pupil, the child has to adjust to the school programme, which is the same for everybody. The new demands are indeed a starting point for new cognitive conquests but also a source of difficulty, disappointment and psychological tension for the child. As a classmate, the child has to deal with its peers, towards whom it may sometimes display cooperative and friendly behaviour, while at other times it displays competitive, aggressive or indifferent behaviour.

Basically, school-age children display an inclination for *productivity* and an inclination to *participate in peer groups*.

With the new knowledge they constantly acquire and with their increasingly developing motor skills, they are called upon to demonstrate that they can undertake and complete activities; to show that they are productive. They test their abilities at different things at home or at school and observe the reactions of the significant people in their lives: their parents and their teachers.

What is demanded of parents at this stage is to observe the changes in their children while at the same time to provide them with the emotional security they need in order to be able to develop their autonomy and their independence over time. For example, a child in the 1st year of primary school can do its "copy" exercises alone, without the help of its parents. Still, children can learn to buy things for themselves, take care of themselves, do housework, work on crafts, cycle and do sports as they acquire kinetic abilities and reinforce their perception.

What can parents do? They can do what Dreikurs said, "Let parents treat children according to their age and their potential."

We should teach them various skills, such as fishing, swimming, how to handle various tools and construction materials as well as to encourage every creative effort they make, whether that means repairing their personal belongings or making constructions on their own. We should show them we have confidence in their abilities and they should feel that they deserve it. We should respect the changes in their personality and trust their abilities for whatever new things they can do now that they could not do before.

In contrast, if we are *overprotective* parents, our children will get the message that they can't manage on their own and will feel weak and disadvantaged. This attitude will not be beneficial to them in school or in their lives. If we tell our children that we will help them get dressed in the morning so that they won't be late for school, or that we will pack their schoolbag for them so that they don't forget anything, or that they should not buy anything from the school canteen because they can't handle money, we contribute to their creating a poor image of themselves. Therefore, they will be afraid to do things on their own, because of their fear of failure. And most likely, they will experience future failures, not because they are not capable, but because they don't feel able to fly with their own wings.

We will produce the same feeling if we are *demanding* as parents; that is, if we make excessive demands on our children, demands they cannot meet. For example, we may want to teach them the multiplication tables before they go to school, we may expect a first-year-primary-school pupil to make no spelling mistakes, when spelling is a skill that is acquired and improved upon throughout primary school, we may demand 4th year pupils to write literary compositions when they have not yet developed their vocabulary skills.

We should not make unreasonable demands on our children because they will start to feel inferior and discouraged, they will have difficulty with their school lessons and they will not be able to perform to their full potential.

We should encourage our children to do whatever they can for their age. What we should tell them is that they are competent enough to do what the school asks of them and that we will support and help them whenever they need our help. In this way, we better respond to our role, which is that of parent-supporter.

In addition, the participation of the child in peer groups may act as a correcting factor for peculiarities that may exist within the family. For example, it may act as a factor that normalises the behaviour of its parents. For example, if parents are biased in favour of their child and have no social measures with which to objectively judge their child's abilities in and out of school, it does not mean that the child will receive the same treatment from its peers. On the contrary, the child will have to conquer everything anew, as far as its relationship with peers is concerned.

Childhood Friendships — Peer Groups

A childhood friendship is a close and intense emotional relationship that the child feels toward one or more children. This relationship is particularly important for the psychological health of the child and contributes to its socialisation at school and in the wider environment.

Children may play with their friends, share a desk at school, study together, spend time at each other's home and so on. In the company of peers, they learn to control their behaviour, to share feelings, to discover themselves through their friends, whom they like and resemble. They also learn to obey rules; otherwise, they are not loved and accepted by teammates. Childhood friendships are a sign and criterion of good mental health and a well-adjusted child.

This is the period when the most beautiful friendships are established, some of which last for years and some for a few weeks; this does not mean that the bond is not strong, however long the friendship lasts. Over time, friendships become more stable, as do the child's interests.

Usually the groups are same-sex; girls hang out with girls and boys with boys. That's because children are trying to acquire and stabilise the behaviour that represents their gender.

The peer groups are basically playgroups. Therefore, if we ask children what they do with their friends and classmates, the only answer they are likely to give us is, "We play". This group, however, is something more: it is the reference group to which the child turns to for behaviour role modelling. From age six, children constantly oppose the views of parents and teachers about what is right or wrong, good or bad, according to their friends' opinions. They gradually take into account not only the opinion of their mother and father but also the views of their peers. A typical example is when the child insists on wearing something other than what its mother has picked out for him.

In the early school years, children's groups have a fluidity and looseness in their organisation. The size of the school group can vary randomly without disrupting the joint activities, nor does gender play a role in this. It is towards the end of primary school that games become more organised, with rules and coordinated actions and groups differentiated by gender; they become same-sex groups. School-age children do not show a strong interest in the opposite sex, but this does not mean that they are not interested at all. The missing element at this age is the sexual feeling, which is why this period – from 9 to 12 years of age – is ideal for the inclusion of sex education in the school curriculum.

Over time, the child's participation in the group becomes more significant. Between the ages of ten and thirteen, children display a great willingness to comply with the rules and team behaviour patterns. They imitate what clothes to wear, what to eat, what sports activities to do, and what games to play. The only thing we can do as observers is to express our views without creating an issue of conflict with their friends, which can lead to reactions and extreme situations.

It is of great importance that, during this period, children form friendships and enjoy their involvement in the group. We should worry only if our child does not want to socialise with anyone and has no friends. We should look into this matter and ask ourselves whether we have offered, on our part, a healthy environment for our child to develop similar behaviour, i.e. whether we helped build its self-confidence, instilled the value of friendship and encouraged its inclusion in a peer group.

WHAT IS THE MOST APPROPRIATE BEHAVIOUR
ON THE PART OF PARENTS?

It is important to know the different ways in which most children perceive and interpret situations and events concerning their group of friends, which is a necessary part of their psychosocial development. If the child does not have this personal sensitivity toward its peer group, it will enter puberty and later adult life with emotional and social gaps. In addition, it will face difficulties in its intimate relationships with the opposite sex.

We should encourage our children to make friends and keep them. They will succeed if we instil in our children values such as a desire to share material goods, ideas, compassion and a willingness to help others, as well as solidarity. By cultivating their emotional intelligence, we can encourage them to learn to act without hurting their fellow human beings, to make mutual concessions and to respect the desire of others.

It is, therefore, a matter of upbringing and our behaviour toward our children that makes the difference.

We must not forget that, as we have repeatedly said, we must show them the way by setting an example with the relationships within the family. If these relationships are democratic, based on mutual respect, solidarity and a genuine interest in one another, the children will try to replicate them in their own relationships with their friends. If we are sociable, organise gatherings and parties, or exchange visits with parents of other children, we help our children open up and make friends more easily.

We should always keep in mind that the child we see growing up in front of our eyes is a small person with needs, aspirations, goals, who is trying to develop his own personality. What we can do is respect the effort he is making and inspire values in him which will help him find his own place in society.

CHAPTER 6

Summer Holidays

WE ALL WANT TO KEEP OUR CHILDREN BUSY during the summer holidays with creative hobbies. Whether they are at camp or at home, there are always opportunities – as long as we take full advantage of them.

One of the best brain exercises for children is reading books during the summer. Follow these steps to get ideas and urge your children to develop good habits during the holidays.

- *Give incentives.* Children love rewards. If there is some kind of reward when they finish reading a good book during the summer, they are more likely to read, and more importantly, it will further ignite their desire to read. You're the one who knows your children so you can find what they are most likely to get excited about.

These incentives can be a day trip to a water park, a visit to an exhibition they are interested in – i.e. a fishing and diving exhibition, an exhibition with expensive cars – a visit to the zoo, the cinema, or something as simple as a rare sticker.

- *Set goals and count points.* Help your children – depending on their age – to set reading as a summer goal. You can monitor their progress and add points depending on the stage they are at. For example, each chapter corresponds to 5 points. You can encourage your children to collect points by reading a book faster. After all, if there is more than one child in the family, competition can work wonders. But make sure to give them a prize or to recognise what they have accomplished when they reach their goals.

- *Let the children choose their own books.* Visit the local library or bookstore with your children; tell them that you will need some time to choose a book you are going to read in the summer and suggest they do the same. When your children see how interested you are in books, and how much time you devote to choosing the right one, they will want to follow your example. Let them choose their own books to read in the summer. When children choose their own books, they are more interested in reading them.

- *Set a reading time.* Whether it is in the morning before starting their day or before the siesta or half an hour before bedtime, set a specific time for reading that fits into your children's daily routine.

- *Encourage children to choose a book series.* Show interest and enthusiasm for books that are part of a series and appropriate for your child's age group. Books that are part of a series arouse a child's interest and children look forward to ending one so as to move on to the next in the series. By starting a new series at the beginning of the summer and encouraging its completion by the end of summer we motivate our children to spend the whole period of their holidays summer with the companionship of a book.

- *Avoid putting pressure on your children to revise for school.* Children need time to discharge from school-work and it is understandable that they will not express any desire, especially in the early days of the holiday, to deal with schoolwork. However, depending on the child (if it is deemed necessary) a ten-minute revision of spelling, multiplication or math helps. One can find books specifically for this purpose in bookshops. (*Porpora* at www.about.com)

CHAPTER 7

Transition from Primary to Secondary School

PRIMARY SCHOOL COMES TO AN END and, in a short time, your child will move on to the next level of education, which is secondary school. How does the child adapt to the new reality? How does it get information about it?

Research has shown that a significant percentage of children going from primary to secondary school find it extremely difficult to adjust to the new school environment for a long time.

It has been observed that the emotions of students who are in secondary school are more intense, resulting in increased displays of pleasure as well as fear and caution. Their negative feelings have to do with "losing their friends" and "taking exams", especially the frequent surprise quizzes and unannounced test, which are not a common occurrence in primary school.

FACTORS AFFECTING THE TRANSITION

Financial, family, social and even health problems, when accumulated, determine how smooth the transition from primary to secondary school will be. Research has shown that by Christmas, that is four months after the start of the school year, 88% of children will have adapted to the new environment.

According to research, children who perform better academically adapt to change more easily. Perhaps these children come from a family environment that is more accepting, more positive towards education. However, this is not the main criterion. The major cause of adjustment difficulties is the child's perpetuation of immaturity. For this reason, it is important for the student to become independent of its parents as concerns studying for school. The student should be able to understand himself and assume the responsibility of studying on his own. Parents should be as consistent and constant as possible in this process.

Secondary school is a difficult transition period because, among other things, it includes subjects that are different from those of primary school. The use of more complex vocabulary also proves difficult for those who find themselves in a very different environment from that of primary school. Many students begin to adjust only after the month of February.

The transition, as we have seen, is not a simple process of changing environments. It is a significant adjustment process that requires delicate cognitive, social and emotional handling in order to help students pass from one phase of their life to another with the least possible difficulty.

PARENTAL ATTITUDES.

The greatest responsibility of the smooth transition of children from primary to secondary school falls on the parents. The changes are great and many and have to do with the personality of the child, who at this stage is going through the period of adolescence, as well as the academic material the student will have to assimilate.

Regarding the child's personality, what parents should do is cultivate their child's self-confidence and boost its self-image. In other words, if they acknowledge and praise its achievements, appreciate its skills and create opportunities for more success, then the child will have greater self-esteem. The child's self-esteem, high or low, is a key factor in shaping its character and personality. Therefore, when we talk about correctly preparing the child for the transition from primary to secondary school, we mean reinforcing the positive image that the child has of itself.

Attending secondary school is the basis for the transition from childhood to adolescence. We must remember that development is built on what already exists. So much depends on the experiences that the child carries from a younger age. If the child is suppressed at its present age in primary school, and is experiencing negative emotions (conflict, oppression, punishment, failure, rejection), then logically speaking, we should expect difficulties and problems in secondary school.

Secondary school and the integration of the child are directly linked to what we as parents and, of course, the school have been preparing for all these years. The better the preparation from early on, the less painful the transition from one stage to another will be. What does this preparation involve? Creating and maintaining good relations, dialogue, contact and communication, mutual respect, humour, acceptance.

In brief, personality traits that we have patiently cultivated in the child all these years. (A. Koptsis & A. Nakos in http://stavgros.files.wordpress.com/2011/07/12-h-didaktiki-twn-thetikwn-epistimwn.pdf)

CHAPTER 8

School Adjustment Difficulties

CHILDREN USUALLY HAVE A POSITIVE ATTITUDE towards school. Parents, kindergarten teachers and other members in their environment prepare them to go to the "big" school. They eagerly await this great moment because, as they have heard, going to school will make them more important because they will learn to do great things. And despite all the protests we usually hear in the beginning, i.e. "Why do I have to wake up so early?" "We have to study from noon till night!" "We have to write so much every day!" attending school is actually a very positive experience for the child.

But there are exceptions to the general rule above. From research conducted on problematic behaviour of children in primary school, it has been found that 10% (6% boys and 4% girls) do not like school. This phenomenon is a result of an interaction of several factors whose causes we will try to present and analyse in simple words, and suggest ways that parents can deal with it. (Paraskevopoulos, 1985 3rd Volume)

This problematic behaviour is usually manifested in the following ways:

- The child manifests antisocial behaviour, that is to say, it expresses aggression, disobedience, negativism, a destructive attitude, restlessness, jealousy, argumentativeness, tension, hyperactivity, rude and insolent behaviour.

- The child may manifest introversion, e.g. does not feel at ease, feels embarrassed, remorse, cries easily, is shy, self-conscious, antisocial, overly-sensitive, easily hurt, has stress, phobias, does not collaborate easily, frightens easily, is absorbed in its own world and is listless.

- The child displays immature or inappropriate behaviour. That is to say, it exhibits behaviour appropriate to a child of a younger age. It may exhibit attention deficit, lack of self-confidence, feelings of inferiority; it may easily get carried away by others, be clumsy or tell lies. In this category, we usually find children with various mild developmental deviations, sensory abnormalities, borderline mental deficiency and specific developmental learning disorders that are usually not identified in time and have serious negative effects on the child's adjustment and progress in school.

- The child may exhibit signs of a psychosomatic disorder, such as skin allergies, dizziness, nausea, vomiting, fearfulness, restlessness, or tics.

Unfortunately, in many countries, the sole criterion used to determine a child's readiness concerning school is its biological age, which often does not coincide with the corresponding maturity needed to attend school. For this reason, the child may need intervention later on when the problem becomes evident, and when the child is already overburdened with obligations and responsibilities above and beyond its abilities to cope. In some countries, however, such as the United Kingdom, children from kindergarten to secondary school can attend classes that correspond to their school maturity, i.e. various school levels (A,B,C) which they have been assigned to after psychometric and cognitive assessment. The content of the material to be taught is designated for each corresponding school level. (Paraskevopoulos, 1985 3rd Volume)

WHEN IS PROBLEMATIC BEHAVIOUR CONSIDERED SERIOUS?

Before concluding that a certain kind of behaviour is serious and dangerous and therefore needs special treatment, we must take the following into account.

A certain kind of behaviour may be a normal reaction of a certain age. This means that it may be a behaviour that will cease to exist in the next developmental stage without affecting the child's mental health. For example, in families where the mother is overprotective, the child senses this bond created by the mother's behaviour, and when the time to part from her comes, it becomes anxious and exhibits school refusal. When the mother encourages the child to acquire autonomy and independence in order to move on to the next stage of its development, this feeling of fear will cease manifesting itself. Therefore, we cannot label this behaviour as "problematic" as it is a direct result of how the parents have handled the situation. However, if this dependency continues to manifest itself at a later stage, i.e. at the age of 7 or 8 years of age, we should be concerned.

Behaviours that appear normal and ideal, for example, a child who always obeys, is timid at school and at home should worry us because the characteristics of this typical school age behaviour is mobility, intense activity, and reaction. Therefore, special attention should be paid to this kind of behaviour because it may be the manifestation of a pathological condition.

Also, any potential problematic behaviour must be examined in connection with the child's environment and its particular personality. We have repeatedly stated that children grow up within the framework set by parents. If parents feed their child negative attitudes or create a negative family environment, it is likely that their children will exhibit the same behaviour.

Domestic violence, aggressive behaviour from family members, lack of parental care, rejection by parents, false expectations, parents with psychological problems, marital conflicts, and hostility between spouses will affect children much more negatively than those caused by common family arguments. Therefore, because every child is different and every family unit is unique, examination of behaviour that worries us should always take the characteristics of the family into account as well as the following:

- Special family circumstances, such as single-parent families, financial problems, authoritarian parents, overprotective parents, family constellation (birth order).

- Adequate parental care (child receives proper nutrition, sleep, medical care and its psychological needs for affection, love, parental recognition, etc. are met).

- Congruity between the biological/physical and mental development of the child. Are there signs of intellectual disability? Are the child's height, weight and motor skills developing normally? Is the child attended to by a paediatrician? Are its vision and hearing checked regularly?

In the event that the problematic behaviour stems from the above, it is obvious that measures should be taken to reduce the phenomena that lead to such behaviour.

Once the above factors have been taken into account and have been eliminated as likely causes, we should be concerned about problematic behaviour when:

- It appears very frequently: The child is often aggressive without any apparent reason in whatever environment it is in.

- It simultaneously exhibits other problems in behaviour, for example, aggressive and antisocial behaviour.

- It deviates from normal behaviour to a high degree. The more behaviour deviates from normal levels, the more serious it is.

- There is a sudden change in the child's behaviour or performance – the child was performing well academically and was interested in his schoolwork and then there was a sharp decline.

- The child seems unable to avoid problematic behaviour. That is, the child cannot adopt proper behaviour.

- When the problematic behaviour hinders cognitive development. For example, the child is distracted and unable to concentrate in school; these problems are often accompanied by hyperactivity and attention-seeking behaviour, which in turn hinders its progress in school. (Paraskevopoulos, 1985, 3rd Volume)

PSYCHOLOGICAL AND CONDUCT DISORDERS

For the purpose of this study and according to the *ICD-10 (International Classification of Diseases, 2008 edition, 10th revision)* and the *National Joint Committee on Learning Disabilities* in the USA (Hamill, 1987 as cited in Papadatos, 2010), we present the phenomena related to:

　　a. Disorders of psychological development

　　b. Learning Disabilities – Specific developmental disorders of scholastic skills

　　c. Disorders of behaviour and emotion with childhood onset

A. Disorders of Psychological Development

The disorders included in this category have the following common characteristics:

1. They typically manifest early in development, during infancy or early childhood.

2. Impairment or delay in development of functions are strongly related to biological maturation of the central nervous system

3. They have a steady course without remissions and relapses. In most cases, the functions affected include language, visuo-spatial skills, and motor coordination. Usually, the delay or impairment diminishes progressively as the child grows older, although milder deficits often remain in adult life.

a. Specific developmental disorders of speech and language

Disorders that appear in the early stages of development. The conditions cannot be directly attributable to neurological or speech mechanism abnormalities, sensory impairments, mental retardation, or environmental factors. Specific developmental disorders of speech and language are often followed by associated problems, such as difficulties in reading and spelling, abnormalities in interpersonal relationships, and emotional and behavioural disorders.

b. Specific speech articulation disorder

Specific developmental disorder in which the use of speech sounds is below the appropriate level for its mental age, but there is a normal level of language skills. Phonological disorder, dyslalia and stuttering belong to this category.

1. Phonological disorder

Children with this disorder have difficulty articulating and producing sounds like *r, s, l*. The disorder often runs in the family, with members displaying difficulties in expression and reception. It occurs in preschool children but in many cases, the symptoms resolve by age nine. (Shriberg, 1999 as cited by Papadatos, 2010).

It is detected when the child does not produce, does not use, does not express and doesn't organise sounds properly and when it substitutes one sound for another, i.e. *f* instead of *th* or omits sounds, i.e. final consonants.

2. Stuttering

Stuttering is a speech disorder that belongs to the developmental disorders and has genetic, psychological and behavioural causes (Yairi & Ambrose, 2004 as cited in Papadatos, 2010). In this disorder, the normal flow and regulation of speech is detuned and the child repeats sounds, syllables and words. The disorder usually begins in early childhood (from two to four years of age) and peaks at age three or four. More specifically, the child may:

- repeat sounds and syllables

- prolong sounds

- make interjections

- pause within a word

- replace words with others to avoid the problematic ones

- produce words with an excess of physical tension

- repeat whole words (e.g., "I-I-I-I see him")

c. Expressive language disorder

A specific developmental disorder in which the child's ability to use expressive spoken language is markedly below the appropriate level for its mental age, but in which language comprehension is within normal limits. There may or may not be abnormalities in articulation. (ICD-10)

Children with this disorder have poor vocabulary and difficulties in learning new words; they use simple sentence structures, omit parts of a sentence, and avoid complex expressions. They also have a slow rate of speech. (Papadatos, 2010)

d. Receptive language disorder

It is a specific developmental disorder in which the child's understanding of language is below the appropriate level for its mental age. In virtually all cases expressive language will also be markedly affected and abnormalities in word-sound production are usual. It is closely related to deficient auditory perception (ICD-10).

B. Learning Difficulties - Specific Developmental Disorders of Scholastic Skills

Learning difficulties are evident in the school process. However, because they are approached by scientists from different disciplines, the focus depends on their area of expertise. That is why terminology and definitions differ, often resulting in disagreement and confusion as to the nature of learning disabilities.

However, the term "learning disability" was accepted after a six-year interdisciplinary study conducted by the *National Joint Committee of Learning Disabilities* in the USA. (Hamill, 1987 as cited in Papadatos, 2010)

According to the above council, "Learning disabilities is a general term that refers to a heterogeneous group of disorders manifested by significant difficulties in the acquisition and use of listening, speaking, reading, writing, reasoning, or mathematical abilities. These disorders are intrinsic to the individual, presumed to be due to central nervous system dysfunction. Although learning disabilities may occur concomitantly with other conditions of deficiency (such as sensory impairment, mental retardation, serious emotional disturbance), they are not the result of those conditions or influences."

Regarding the cause, the focus is on the dysfunction of the central nervous system, through which intrinsic learning processes and use of information are determined. It may also occur across the life span of the individual. Given that reading is a complex cognitive skill that requires the recognition and differentiation of visual stimuli, the lack of this skill is responsible for the manifestation of one type of reading difficulty, *dyslexia*.

A student is considered to have this disorder when its reading skills are one or two years below what would be expected for the child's chronological age (Kaplan & Sadock, 1985 as cited in Papadatos, 2010). But it is not correct or beneficial to wait in order to see and to verify this difficulty. We will never be able to counterbalance the numerous failures that will have accumulated in the meantime, nor all the negative effects that will have shaped the child's personality.

Therefore, the possible areas of deficiency should be identified as early as possible so as not to create learning problems in the future.

The characteristics of dyslexia are usually detected in the first three or four years of primary school. The difficulties in the areas of reading (mainly), writing and spelling are as follows:

- Adds and / or removes letters, syllables, and words.

- confuses letters that look alike: p - q, b - d.

- confuses letters that sound alike: g-j, q-k.

- reverses letters or syllables such as dat instead of bat.

- Repeats letters, syllables, and words.

- Has problems with stress, intonation, punctuation.

- Often loses its place in the text.

- Reads slowly (syllabic reading).

- The child's reading ability is not consistent with its level
   of intelligence and reading training it has received.

The psychosocial problems created as a result of this disorder are
the focus of increasingly more studies. According to Harris & Sipay
(1980), these problems are:

- conscious refusal to learn

- negative conditioning to reading

- aggressiveness

- displacement of aggressiveness

- resistance to pressure

- tendency to be dependent

- quick discouragement

- conviction that success is dangerous

- disruptive behaviour or restlessness

- absorption in a private world

(Tzouriadou, 2008)

While the *National Joint Committee of Learning Disabilities* in the US
(Hamill, 1987 as cited in Papadatos, 2010) interprets the term "learning
disabilities" as 'disturbances resulting from severe difficulties in learning
and use of speech, reading, writing, logical thinking and mathematical abilities' the *ICD-10* (*International statistical classification of diseases
and related health problems*, version 2008, 10th revision) uses the term
"specific developmental disorders of scholastic skills" to describe related

disorders, in which the normal patterns of skill acquisition are disturbed from the early stages of development. It does not refer to it as a consequence of a lack of learning opportunities, or result of intellectual disability or some form of brain injury or damage.

The *ICD-10* classifies the developmental disorders of scholastic skills into the following types:

a. Specific reading disorder (developmental dyslexia)

The main feature of this disorder is a specific and significant impairment in the development of reading skills that is not solely accounted for by mental age, visual acuity problems, or inadequate schooling. Reading comprehension skill, reading word recognition, oral reading skill, and performance of tasks requiring reading may all be affected. Spelling difficulties are frequently associated with specific reading disorders and often remain well into adolescence even if there is now some progress in reading. It is usually preceded by a history of disorders in speech and language. (ICD-10)

b. Specific spelling disorder

The main feature is a specific and significant impairment in the development of spelling skills in the absence of a history of specific reading disorder, which is not solely accounted for by low mental age, visual acuity problems, or inadequate schooling. The ability to spell orally and to write out words correctly are both affected.

c. Disorder of written expression (dysorthographia, dysgraphia)

This disorder is characterised by a reduced ability of the child to compose a written text. The reduced ability is evident by the abundance of spelling errors (dysorthographia), errors in grammar, poor organisation of paragraphs and very bad handwriting (dysgraphia).

The diagnostic criteria in *DSM-IV* for the disorder of written expression is:

1. Writing skills, as measured by individually administered standardised tests (or functional assessments of writing skills), are substantially below those expected given the person's chronological age, measured intelligence, and age-appropriate education.

2. The disturbance in Criterion A significantly impedes school performance or activities of daily living that require the composition of written texts (e.g., writing grammatically correct sentences and organised paragraphs).

3. If a sensory deficit is present, the difficulties in writing skills are in excess of those usually associated with it.

The disorder often coexists with a reading disorder (dyslexia) or disorder of arithmetical skills (dyscalculia). It rarely displays itself on its own. The disorder usually becomes evident in the second year of primary school (which is typically preceded by the teaching of sentence structure), and sometimes later on.

Many times, poor handwriting (dysgraphia) is due to difficulties with motor coordination (dyspraxia), therefore it falls under the category of *specific developmental disorders of motor function*. (American Psychiatric Association, 1994)

d. Specific disorder of arithmetical skills (dyscalculia)

It is a specific impairment in arithmetical skills that cannot be explained solely on the basis of general mental retardation or of inadequate schooling. It is more about learning the basic computational skills of addition, subtraction, multiplication and division, rather than comprehension of more abstract mathematical concepts required in algebra, trigonometry, geometry, or mathematics.

The mathematical disorder usually becomes evident in the first years of primary school and consists of a lack of understanding of mathematical concepts, difficulty in executing mathematical equations or recognising mathematical symbols. We see this when the child's performance deviates from what is expected for its age and educational level in relation to its cognitive level. Usually, children with mathematics disorders have difficulties in visuo-spatial and visual perceptual abilities.

e. Mixed disorder of scholastic skills

These are disorders in which both arithmetical skills and reading or spelling skills are significantly impaired, but in which the disorder is not solely explicable in terms of general mental retardation or of inadequate schooling.

THE ROLE OF THE FAMILY IN DEALING WITH CHILDREN WITH LEARNING DIFFICULTIES

Concerning the role of the family in dealing with children with learning difficulties, Susana Panteliadis states *the following* (Panteliadis & Boccia, 2007. Chap. 3: Families with children with learning difficulties, p. 16-17):

"The family is a system of relationships among its members, but also a part of other wider systems. So, whatever happens in a family, its reaction and the consequences of its reaction forms a composition of variables, where interactions are constantly active. In addition, each family tries to adapt to the particular environment in which it lives, through the interaction of cultural values, its objectives and the specific characteristics of the environment. The needs of the family and parents are not always the same, but are formed according to the family's stage of development, and in relation to how aware they are of the fact that their child has a learning disability. Although parents go through specific stages when they discover their child has a problem, they don't all go through the stages in the same manner. According to this systemic view, every family has its own characteristics, interactions, functions and level of evolution and therefore is unique.

❧   ❧

When the family has a child with learning difficulties, the most critical moment is when the learning disability is recognised and diagnosed in the child, which usually occurs after the commencement of school. At this point, when the parents discover that their hitherto perfectly normal child has a serious problem, they may feel anger, disappointment, or experience physical symptoms. Another very common reaction is to search for other specialists to dismiss or confirm the diagnosis. It is expected and acceptable for parents to look for a second opinion, particularly in the case of learning disabilities, which is difficult to diagnose at an early age. With regard to the use of defence mechanisms, this may prove useful in the first phase as they provide an opportunity for parents to adjust. Otherwise, parents may react by coming into conflict with their partner, by consulting numerous specialists hoping for a different diagnosis or by resorting to a series of defence mechanisms such as denial (Gallagher, 1995).

After the initial adjustment (whether effective or not), the parents try to comprehend the causes and seek likely treatments. The parents seek the causes, either in order to rid themselves of feelings of guilt or in order to find the suitable treatment. Regarding their emotional reaction, parents either accept their child with learning difficulties or reject it. In the case of acceptance, the parents focus on the positive points and on the progress and do not dwell on the failures. On the contrary, in the case of rejection, certain parents may make unrealistic demands that prevent the optimal growth of the child or may overprotect it by overly decreasing their demands or, still, they try to cover up the rejection with excessively positive comments.

At this particular point, the role of the teacher is exceptionally important. The provision of objective information and the discreet but constant support can facilitate the parents in the choice of suitable social services and in making correct educational decisions.

> *When the parents accept their child who has learning difficulties, they focus on the positive points and on the progress and do not dwell on the failures. In the opposite case, they make unrealistic demands that prevent the optimal growth of the child or they overprotect it by overly decreasing their demands and expressing excessively positive comments.*

In the field of learning disabilities, from when this subject first came to light, parents have played an important role and have had great influence, to the extent that they were actively engaged in the recognition of learning disabilities as a category of special educational needs.

Furthermore, research findings have highlighted the importance of the role of the families of children with learning disabilities both in understanding the problems arising (Toro, Weissberg, Guare & Liebenstein, 1990) as well as for the support they offer (Miedel & Reynolds, 2000; Temple, & Miedel Reynolds, 2000; Eiserman, Weber & McCoun, 1995). More specifically, research suggests that increasing the frequency of contact between teachers and parents, increases the positive attitude of one group towards the other and interventions at school are more effective if accompanied by supporting parents at home (Michael, Arnold, Magliocca & Miller, 1992).

C. *Disorders of Behaviour and Emotion*

a. Attention Deficit - Hyperactivity Disorder (ADHD)

Usually children are characterised by excessive activity, energy and carelessness in their movements. It is typical of their age, as they develop from one stage to another. In other words, these behaviours accompany their psychosocial development during preschool and primary school.

As children grow, we expect to see them maturing as to the above behaviours. We expect them to be calmer and more organised; to pay attention and to concentrate more on what they are doing; to be more dedicated to school and to extracurricular activities, which include their homework, various school projects, regular participation in sports; to organise their personal belongings; to show self-control, etc.

So, if instead of this behaviour, we see that the child loses interest in things faster than other children, is often "out of control", is easily distracted by external stimuli and exhibits other symptoms that will be discussed below, we must look deeper into the matter.

The symptoms of Attention Deficit - Hyperactivity Disorder (ADHD) usually appear at the young age of 3-6 years, but because they vary or may coexist in combination with other symptoms, ADHD is difficult to diagnose.

Teachers can more easily observe symptoms of hyperactivity, inattention and impulsivity because they are directly associated with the first basic skills to be acquired by the child entering primary school. If our child performs poorly in reading in the first year, we will need to consult and cooperate with the teacher.

How well a child cooperates with others in class shows its level of self-control and impulsivity. Hyperactive children are not liked by others and are often isolated or, conversely, trying in various unconventional ways to draw the attention of their classmates and teachers. Thus, a vicious circle is created where the child experiences feelings of reduced self-esteem resulting in difficult contact with the environment.

Children with Attention Deficit-Hyperactivity Disorder (ADHD) do not really follow the teacher's instructions or the classroom rules and are often "distracted" during the course of the lesson. What's more, 50-60% of children with ADHD have significant learning difficulties. These difficulties, combined with others that are created along the way if there is no intervention/treatment, result in a higher rate of 'flunking' or staying in the same class, that in other children without the disorder. Some even drop out of school once they complete the first three years of secondary school (Manuzza et al., 1997 from Zafiropoulou & Kalantzi-Azizi, 2011).

DIAGNOSIS OF ADHD

For early diagnosis of ADHD, there is no particular test that shows if a child actually has ADHD. Usually parents consult the paediatrician or the teacher, who recommends a school psychologist. In any case, the mental health specialist usually takes other possible causes into account and advises parents to check the child for:

- an ear infection that may have affected hearing
- impaired vision that has gone undetected
- anxiety or depression or other psychiatric problems that have symptoms similar to ADHD

- a health problem that affects attention and behaviour

- major alterations in their lives such as the death of a family member, a divorce under extreme and bad conditions, job loss of parents, etc.

The above constitute temporary behaviours in children, which can look like behaviours caused by ADHD. However, if these causes are excluded, the mental health specialist moves on and requests information from parents and teachers. The specialist examines whether the school and family environment are problematic or particularly stressful. He closely monitors the child's behaviour in different situations. The specialist also consults the teacher about the child's behaviour in relation to its level of intelligence and the presence of other learning difficulties.

Then, in order to complete the screening and get official confirmation of the presence or not of this disorder, the mental health expert refers parents to the appropriate *state assessment centres*, which can certify the severity of the disorder and prescribe special education and monitoring of the child by a special educator, who should work closely with the school and parents.

CAUSES OF ADHD

According to studies (Hinshaw, 1994; Barkley, 1997 by Zafiropoulou & Kalantzi-Azizi, 2011), the causes of the development of this disorder are the following:

1. Genetic

Surveys and studies on biological and adoptive parents of children with ADHD in twins and half siblings reveal the hereditary nature of the disorder but have not yet found sufficient evidence of chromosomal abnormalities. When there is a biological parent with the disorder, the chances of the child manifesting the disorder may reach up to 57% (Biederman et al., 1999 as cited in Papadatos, 2010). Also, siblings of hyperactive children are at higher risk of displaying problems.

The speed of conversion as well as the levels of glucose in the blood (fuel of the organism) are considered of primary importance in the activity of psychological functions. Glucose is a fundamental source of energy for the brain, and consequently, its availability influences psychological activities. When glucose levels are low, the psychological processes that require intellectual effort (e.g. self-monitoring, decision-making) are reduced. The blood flow in the brain has been investigated using the PET (positron emission tomography) scan in parents with children that have ADHD in order to measure the rate of change and the levels of glucose in the blood, and it was discovered that both the conversion rate as well as the levels of glucose were low.

2. Brain growth and function

In research using magnetic resonance imaging (MRI), differences were found in the frontal lobes that are located anterior to the central brain fissures. These lobes play an essential role in the planning and the execution of behaviours that result from learning and intention. Also, it is the seat of response inhibition and consequently, if there is a dysfunction in this part of the brain, we see an inability to guide behaviour based on internally processed information and reduced psychomotor control, which result in the three symptoms of ADHD, that is to say, lack of attention, impulsivity and hyperactivity.

Also, neurochemical research has proven the relationship between ADHD and the dopamine active transporter (DAT), which is related with the symptoms of hyperactivity and impulsivity; and with the dopamine receptor D4 (DRD4), that is related more with the symptom of carelessness (Waldman, 1997, Lahoste et al., 1996 as cited in Papadatos, 2010).

3.Family - Social - Environmental

It is important to stress that the behaviour of a child with ADHD is not only due to the above genetic and neurological causes, but is the result of all the influences that have been received during its cognitive and psychosocial development. Insufficient or incorrect upbringing, disturbed marital or family relationships, a lack of support from the family and the school environment contribute to the maintenance of the disorder. (Papadatos, 2010)

TREATING ADHD

The need for prevention and intervention is very high if we wish to promptly address the problem before it becomes worse and leads the child into situations that will complicate the rest of its life. ADHD symptoms continue to manifest themselves in adolescence and adulthood. The hyperactivity turns into a constant feeling of restlessness and, generally, adults with ADHD are unable to organise themselves and set objectives in their academic, professional and personal lives.

The available therapeutic approaches focus primarily on reducing the symptoms of ADHD and improving child and family development and encouraging the interaction between parent and child. Depending on the extent and intensity of the disorder, treatment may consist of medication, various types of psychotherapy, special education, or a combination of the above.

What is certain is that once the symptoms and problems are identified not only at school but also at home, as well as in the broader social environment, therapeutic intervention is a must and requires the coordination and cooperation of all those involved (the mental health specialist, teachers, parents, special education teacher).

What Parents Should Do

Particular emphasis is placed on how involved parents should be and what role they should play as co-educators. That is why parent counselling is especially important. Parents should consult a mental health specialist to help them understand the issue as objectively as possible and to prepare for their role as the parents of a child with special needs.

Apart from the psychological support they may receive, they also learn several useful techniques on how to deal with problematic behaviour. They learn how to implement a system of reward and consequence whose aim is to modify the child's behaviour. They learn to reward behaviours that they want to encourage and ignore or distract children's attention from behaviours they want to avoid. In cases where the child's behaviour is out of control, they apply the method of 'time-out' (social exclusion) and remove the child from the place where the undesirable behaviour occurs.

More specifically, they can help the child by:

- providing it with some personal space where it is not distracted by various objects (toys, computer) that might be in its room. Ideally, it should be a separate study area where the child can do its schoolwork undisturbed.

- keeping to the daily schedule and not changing it. Maintain the same daily routine from morning until night. The schedule should include the required study time and time for outdoor and indoor activities. This timetable should be placed somewhere where it is visible any time of day (i.e. on the refrigerator or on the noticeboard in the kitchen), and any changes should be planned in advance.

- keeping everyday items tidy and organised and

emphasising to the child the usefulness of doing so. Parents should designate a specific place for clothes, schoolbags, books and toys, and should make sure they are always tidy.

- creating a calendar for schoolwork and urging the child to fill it in on its own in order to acquire the habit of planning. The child can note down any details it needs to remember, such as a project deadline or a planned school excursion. The planned excursion is an excellent opportunity because the child can make a list of all it needs for the excursion. In this manner, the child can plan for the day of the excursion and make all the necessary provisions in order to have a good time.

- being clear and consistent with the rules they set. Children with ADHD need more time to understand rules and how they should be applied.

- rewarding and praising their children when they follow the rules that have been set. When this is done consistently, it counteracts the criticism they receive from their environment, or the school (by their classmates) or the wider community (by their peers and their surroundings). The reward can take several forms, i.e. accumulating points (bonus) in order to get a special treat such as going to the cinema or a zoo or places that we know they like a lot.

It is very important for parents to know that, in order to have the desired effect, there should be one direction (the same line) by both parents in applying these rules. The existence of family or marital problems does not help in this direction and should be treated with family therapy beforehand if the problems are significant.

b. Aggressive Behaviour

Aggression is one of the characteristics of behaviour that indicates conduct disorder. According to psychoanalysts, aggression is inherent in human nature, in other words we are born with it. Genetic and biological factors create a predisposition for aggression or antisocial behaviour, but its actual manifestation ultimately depends on the interaction of familial and social factors. (Capaldi & Patterson, 1994 as cited in Zafiropoulou & Kalantzi-Azizi, 2011).

What are the signs of aggressive behaviour? According to the *DSM-IV (Diagnostic Manual of the American Psychiatric Association)*, the repetitive and persistent pattern of behaviour in which the basic rights of others or major age-appropriate societal norms or rules are violated is evidence of the existence of aggressive or delinquent behaviour.

Of course, we are not talking about two-, three,- or four-year old toddlers that exhibit aggressive behaviour when other children take their toys. We would call this "healthy" aggressiveness as it is an attempt to assert themselves and safeguard their rights in a way they see fit at that moment. This reaction is normal because infants have not yet been socialised and may not even realise that their actions cause pain and hurt others. Reactions such as pushing and hitting can be considered developmental characteristics of early childhood.

Aggression as a disorder, as analysed in this chapter, is classified according to its onset. Aggressive behaviour may either appear before the age of 10 or only after the age of 10. The first type has an earlier onset with children exhibiting aggressive behaviour around the age of five or six and is more manifest in late childhood; while the second case specifically refers to aggressive behaviour displayed after 10 years of age, with onset in early adolescence. A child falls into the second type when it has displayed no aggressive behaviour before the age of 10. The age of onset of aggressive behaviour is an important factor indicating the severity of the disorder and its evolutionary path. Children with the early onset type of the disorder are more likely to continue manifesting antisocial behaviour in adulthood in comparison to those with the adolescent-onset type.

The incidence of bullying has increased over recent decades. It is seen more in urban than in rural areas. In research conducted regarding the sex of children, aggressive behaviour is displayed in 6% to 16% in boys and 2% to 9% in girls. This variation depends on the sample population studied as well as the tools used for research.

The symptoms can manifest themselves and be seen as an indication of aggressive behaviour and should be assessed in terms of their duration (weeks, months), frequency of appearance (frequently or sporadically), the severity of the phenomenon (mild, moderate, severe), the context in which it occurs (home, school, friends or everywhere); these symptoms are key factors, and above all, at least three of them must be present simultaneously over a period of 12 months.

The following are examples of the type of aggressive behaviour displayed:

- often bullies, threatens, or intimidates others
- often initiates physical fights
- has used a weapon that can cause serious physical harm to others (e.g., a bat, piece of wood, broken bottle, knife)
- has been physically cruel to people or animals
- has attacked someone in order to steal from him
- has deliberately set fire with the intent to cause serious damage
- has destroyed others' property (other than by fire setting)
- often lies to obtain goods or favours or to avoid obligations
- has stolen items of low value without physically attacking anyone
- is often truant from school, beginning before age 13 years
- has run away from home overnight at least twice without parental permission

(Manos, 1997 as cited in Zafiropoulou & Kalantzi-Azizi, 2011)

It should however be noted that the diagnosis of aggressive behaviour should only be assessed by mental health specialists, whereas the above characteristics are only indications that parents should take into account in order to promptly deal with such a development in the child's behaviour.

It is worth noting here that the early onset of conduct disorder shows comorbidity with attention deficit disorder and with emotional disorders, such as speech disorders or neuropsychological disorders associated with impaired concentration and a low IQ (Moffitt, 1993). In other words, children with a low IQ are more likely to display aggressive behaviour.

Bandura (1991), the main representative of social learning, has highlighted the fact that the existence of aggressive behaviour in children is due to environmental and cognitive factors as well as self-regulatory mechanisms in behaviour. The child learns aggressive behaviour by observing and imitating its role models. Who are these role models? They are the child's significant people in their life, i.e. parents and peers; and role models from the media (television, the internet) and society in general.

Several studies have shown that when the child observes a role model, it learns not only by observing the behaviour of the model but also by observing the consequences of the role model's behaviour. If the role model was punished for his behaviour, the child will not imitate the observed behaviour. By observing, the child learns to self-regulate its behaviour and to act according to cognitive processes it gradually acquires, depending on the education it receives and the objectives set: boosting self-esteem and self-reinforcement or remorse, guilt, shame, and self-punishment.

FAMILY FACTORS

The role of the family, which we see in everything related to the proper development of a child, is a catalyst for the emergence of aggressive behaviour; the first indications of such behaviour are manifested among its members.

Frequent marital conflicts and messy divorces have resulted in an increased incidence of conduct problems in children. While, on the contrary, less marital conflict and more cooperation prevent such phenomena. It is important to emphasise here that the existence of hostility between spouses has a greater negative impact on children than does the mere existence of disagreements. In other words, feelings of hatred, hostility and vengeance are the basic components that are usually hidden behind acts of aggression, which should greatly worry us.

The use of corporal punishment or other coercive methods, such as orders, threats, excessive deprivations, make children feel and behave with hostility towards their parents. Very often, parents act spasmodically, experimenting with different behavioural techniques on their children or their partners, which do not always have the anticipated results. What follows is usually disappointment and anger, which lead to conflicts and sometimes to violence. What is certain is that this behaviour returns to them with the same characteristics and thus a vicious circle is maintained. The children, in turn, become victims of this behaviour and often repeat the same behaviour on their younger siblings, their peers, at home, and at school.

Research has shown that children with aggressive behaviour have themselves been victims of domestic violence or have witnessed violence at home or the consumption of alcohol or other substances by their parents. Basically, when parents display this behaviour, the message conveyed to children is that only with violence do we have the results we want. If, for example, we punish a child using physical force (spanking) because the child hit his friend, we are basically confirming that by hitting someone we are stronger than, we can achieve whatever we want.

Also, the quality of the mother-infant bond has been shown to affect the quality of the child's subsequent relationships and has been linked with the occurrence of conduct disorder in children. According to Bowlby (1973), the reason is that the child who has formed a secure attachment with his mother has developed positive expectations from others, trust in human relations as well as in his personal worth. As a result, the child relates to others in a positive and trusting manner, unlike children who as infants did not form a secure attachment with their mother. A lack of warmth and love from the mother contributes to the development of aggressive behaviour in children.

ENVIRONMENTAL FACTORS

One of the major environmental factors that have been linked to aggressive and antisocial behaviour is poverty. Other factors such as belonging to a large family, parents with a lower educational status, harsh living conditions, etc. also contribute and have a cumulative effect on the manifestation of aggressive behaviour. These phenomena can lead children to develop problems of aggressive and delinquent behaviour as adults.

TELEVISION VIEWING

It is a fact that watching violent scenes affects the emergence of aggressive behaviour. When children watch television programmes containing violent and frightening scenes without limits and without the supervision of their parents, they are more likely to identify with their "heroes" and will try to display similar behaviour by creating scenarios that are stored in memory and affect how they interpret future social stimuli (Vosniadou, 2001). Children who watch violent programmes under the supervision of their parents are less affected by the violent scenes as compared to those who watch these programmes unsupervised by parents. Even the context within which violence is represented significantly affects the child's behaviour. When the hero of the film is not punished for his actions, thus legitimising violence, television viewing has a greater impact on the child's behaviour. That is why it is recommended parents monitor their children's viewing habits and select which programmes their children can watch. Parents should take the time to have discussions about what the kids see on TV and to help them cultivate healthy criteria for judging and comparing behaviours and acts they have seen, so that they can assess them according to the value system they have acquired through proper education.

PEERS

Aggressive children usually experience the rejection of their peers, which creates more problems in their adjustment and is closely associated with increased aggressive behaviour. From various measures, it has been found that aggressive boys who had been rejected by their peers in the 3rd year of primary school became even more aggressive and displayed antisocial behaviour between the 6th year of primary school and the 9th year of secondary school. (Coie et al., 1995 as cited in Zafiropoulou & Kalantzi-Azizi, 2011).

TRAINING PARENTS ON HOW TO DEAL
WITH AGGRESSIVE BEHAVIOUR

When a child exhibits aggressive behaviour, parents should handle it appropriately. If the situation is unsettled, they should immediately remove the child to another room to reduce tension and to calm it down. There they can discuss the causes and consequences of its aggressive conduct. If parents have fostered empathy in the child, they can ask it to put itself in the other child's shoes and to describe how he would have felt if he had been the victim.

Under no circumstances should we punish the child by using either corporal punishment or verbal abuse (i.e. "You're bad, inexcusable," etc.). We always talk about the behaviour: "Your behaviour was un-acceptable, and I fear that if you go on like this you will lose your friend," "How would you feel you if you were in his position and were pushed and fell and hurt yourself?" "I'm sure your friend was really hurt and is upset with what you did!" If we cultivate empathy, then, when it has calmed down, the child will reconsider its behaviour and will probably not repeat it.

We must explain to our children that violence hurts others and that, in order to live harmoniously with others, we should respect people's freedom and physical integrity. We should help them cultivate the skill of self-control and find compromising solutions instead of fighting with their friends and classmates. If we judge that the situation is seri-ous, the withdrawal of some privileges is imperative after explaining to them that we impose them in order to help them understand that this consequence (punishment) is the result of violent behaviour expressed and not because we don't love them.

Also, the more attention we pay to proper education, the more we will prevent such displays of aggression. When we cultivate respect and affection towards the child, it will reciprocate.

However, we must be consistent and we must be able to justify the rules and limits we set for our children by giving reasonable explana-tions both for their existence as well as for the consequences when the rules are broken.

VICTIMISATION-BULLYING (THE OTHER PERSPECTIVE)

Victimisation is the attempted subjugation of one child by another. One child becomes the target of an aggressive child who may be physically or mentally stronger. What do we as parents do to protect our children when they are in this situation and they have to defend themselves?

The most important thing we can teach our children within the family is mutual respect. Always treat children as unique individuals who deserve justice and respect. Teach them to be assertive within the family and outside it. Because assertive children are much more likely to be healthier and happier, more sincere and less manipulative.

Children feel better about themselves when they demand and enjoy equal treatment from their classmates, peers, teachers, parents; this leads to a more active adulthood. They learn to handle difficult or unpleasant situations with directness and honesty without being rude but without allowing the rudeness of others to displease them and make them angry.

With assertiveness training, they learn to express their feelings about an event triggered by the aggressive behaviour of a child.

They learn to defend themselves, to say "no" with a steady gaze where it should, how to respond to criticism or a malicious attack, how to express their anger and defend their views.

They learn to defend their rights and to respond to those who violate these rights or the rights of others, and to demand a safe environment where any manifestation of aggressive behaviour is not accepted.

Example: Katerina took her sister's, Mary's, personal belongings without asking. Mary, looking steadily at Katerina, expresses her feelings of anger by saying:

"Katerina, I am angry about what you did! I really hate it when I can't find my stuff in my wardrobe and I realise that you took it without asking!"

She defends her right for her personal space and her personal things.

"I respect your right to have your personal stuff in your room and they are yours to do whatever you want with them; that's why you should do the same with my things."

She sets limits and suggests ways to treat each other as equals.

"The next time you need something of mine, I would like you to ask for my permission first."

It is important to teach our children appropriate survival techniques and the ability to behave adaptively. The avoidance of victimisation – which is, in effect, the adoption of assertive behaviour – boosts their self-esteem, reduces the anxiety and remorse that accompany passive attitudes, increases the respect for others, as well as improves the ability to communicate effectively with others.

It is vital for the family, the school and other institutions (extra-curricular activities) to treat children as human beings who deserve respect and honour, in the same way they treat adults, and to avoid behaviour that takes advantage of them because of their position and their strength, i.e. parents-teachers (= strong) versus children (=powerless) (Alberti & Emmons, 2008).

c. School refusal – Anxiety

School refusal is manifested in various ways. The child is reluctant to go to school or refuses to leave on time, or right before leaving it manifests psychosomatic symptoms, such as headaches, diarrhoea, stomach aches, or finds some other excuse not to go to school. The reasons it gives may be that the teacher's mean, that his classmates scare and threaten him, the schoolwork is difficult, etc.

We should not confuse school refusal with the child's instinctive reactions towards the unfamiliar and unknown when it starts school, as these reactions start to subside after the first few days of adjustment.

Nor should we associate it with specific events, such as if the child is afraid of a classmate who is threatening to hit him, or is afraid because the teacher will call on him and he is anxious because he has not studied.

School refusal is none of the above. It is a type of psychoneurosis identified by intense psychic anxiety that is not justified by the situation or the level of the child's development. This fear is considered irrational by others in the environment and the child is affected on a daily basis.

Etiologically, school refusal is considered an acute manifestation of permanent separation anxiety (Paraskevopoulos, 1985, 3rd volume). The attachment of the child to the mother appears very early and a strong and close emotional bond between mother-child is quickly formed. The first consequences of this relationship are separation and anxiety, which are considered normal until the child becomes two, but should then begin to subside. However, in this case, it increases and becomes permanent.

The mother's psychological reaction contributes to this because she too feels the same separation anxiety as the child – she also feels lonely and insecure away from the child – but does nothing other than keep the child "psychologically captive" and "doesn't allow it" to go to school. This psychological state is conveyed to the child and the separation anxiety is transferred from the real cause (the removal from the home) to a stimulus (the school) that until recently did not exist. This feeling can intensify when there are difficult and adverse conditions in school, i.e. a strict teacher, a crowded classroom, etc.

In combination with the above, the family conditions in which the child grows up and develops play an important role in its attitude toward the new experience of starting school.

The child's reactions are usually the following:

- The child cries and begs not to be sent to school; it may tremble and shake, and physically resist going.

- In the classroom, it is too shy to speak in front of everyone for fear of making a mistake.

- The child avoids new people and is upset with changes.

- The child has difficulty taking part in group activities in class.

- The child is afraid that it will not make any friends and will be alone.

- The child is afraid that it will not do well on tests and will disappoint its parents and teacher.

- The child is afraid to be separated from its parents.

The child with anxiety:

- worries about the slightest thing;

- is upset with whatever happens;

- asks for confirmation and constantly worries about its abilities;

- always controls its behaviour and often underestimates its abilities;

- focuses more on the details of an issue than the essence, i.e. erasing and rewriting words in order to have a clearly written notebook and not checking the accuracy of the sentences; constantly sharpening his pencil and not solving the equation.

The existence or the repetition of all the above reactions and behaviours puts the child in a permanent state of anxiety and it always feels ill at ease without being able to determine the actual cause. The child always feels its self-image and identity is being threatened.

In fact, children suffer from anxiety and school refusal more frequently than they do from other difficulties adjusting to school. Nevertheless, although parents and teachers quickly identify children with these difficulties, they don't consider them to be very serious problems and do not address the matter promptly.

But the results are significant if the problem is not addressed:

- Children suffer psychologically when psychosomatic disturbances appear (abdominal pains, headaches, etc.).

- They cannot follow the lesson.

- They suffer because they do not want to part with their parents.

- They stay on the sidelines as they do not participate in class activities.

- They are labelled as bad students, which lowers their self-esteem.

That is why, with these phenomena, parents and teachers must act promptly, without wasting time, before the children suffer the consequences.

Regarding parents, we should refer to the way they help their children in their psychosocial development and evolution long before pre-school age. It is important to emphasise that the way a mother deals with the gradual separation from her child is reflected in the child and affects its psychological state and how it will deal with the same matter. The more the mother believes that she has to give the child space to develop its autonomy so as not to suffer psychologically at the thought of separation, the more she helps it to better socialise and integrate more easily into the new environment of the school and of the group, which is a new reality for the child.

Still, when parents gradually grant their children autonomy and do not limit their individuality, they help them feel strong enough to face their minor difficulties. When parents let them take the initiative and recognise their potential, they boost their children's self-esteem making them courageous enough to test their strength. Encouraging children in this direction – always taking the child's temperament into account – reduces the chances of the child developing phobias in the future (see the relevant sub-chapter "Encouraging our Child").

Also, the emotional intelligence that has developed on the parents' side will help them understand and promptly identify the problem, because through this process the child will express its feelings about events and situations, allowing parents to handle the situation properly. The positive attitude of the parents, the emotional warmth, and the sense of security that they convey to the children cultivate the ground for proper psychosocial development without any phobias or anxiety

Parents, however, should not avoid involving themselves in situations that cause them stress and anxiety because they consider them dangerous, for in so doing they cultivate anxiety and phobia in their children. Children grow up in the context set up by their parents. The family attitude toward what is considered hard, dangerous, stressful, and new largely determines how our children will behave in such situations.

The positive expectations expressed by parents toward any attempt of the child act as a protective shield against feelings of fear and low self-esteem. "You are smart and I'm sure you can do it!" "Well done! The effort was great!" In this way, we boost the child's confidence and it is not afraid to try again in the event of failure.

Parents who teach their children to face difficult situations by showing their strength and courage prove more effective than parents who tend to overprotect their children in various difficult circumstances and problems. These children gain comparatively more experience, which facilitates their development.

Practically speaking, if the child displays school refusal, and after parents have come into contact with the teacher to examine the child's activities throughout the school day, even during the breaks, they should consistently apply the following techniques:

a. They must explain to the child that not going to school is out of the question.

b. They shouldn't pay particular attention to complaints of physical symptoms, which seem to disappear once the child stays home.

c. If the child does not go to school one time, there is no need to reinforce this behaviour. In other words, the child should not be allowed to watch its favourite movie, or sleep longer. Instead, parents need to discuss school and its obligations with the child and have the child take responsibility for its refusal to go to school and answer the following questions: What justification will be given to the school for its absence? How will it deal with questions from its classmates? How will it make up for the lessons it has missed?

d. They must make sure the morning routine of getting ready for school is not stressful. This means either arriving at school early, before all the other pupils have gathered in the schoolyard, or a little later and before the bells rings.

e. Upon its return from school, the child should be praised for its efforts, even if it did not feel well at school and requested to leave.

d. Childhood Timidity, Shyness, Introversion, and Loneliness

There are children who are timid and shy. Sometimes children display such high levels of timidity that they become alienated from their social environment.

Timidity is a feeling that causes embarrassment and fear towards people or towards different social situations. It is more evident when the person has to face new situations or when they are being judged. It can be permanent or occasional, i.e. it can be a permanent feature of one's personality or only appear, for example, when someone has to speak in front of an audience or finds oneself among strangers. Several factors contribute to the manifestation of this emotional reaction (Zafiropoulou & Kalantzi-Azizi, 2011).

Natural shyness is a normal feature of infancy and childhood, and perhaps the beginning of adolescence. Over time, and inasmuch as the child grows and acquires social skills, both feelings of shyness and timidity subside. This happens to a large extent when the child acquires preschool education (kindergarten, nursery schools), a phenomenon more common in urban areas rather than in rural areas, because it helps the child acquire social and other experiences before starting school.

WHAT FACTORS CONTRIBUTE TO THE MAINTENANCE OF TIMIDITY IN CHILDREN?

- *A lack of confidence* and fear of failure. Some kids are frustrated by their early school failures. They feel they cannot meet the demands of school, especially when they are not supported psychologically by their parents or their teachers. So they give up and "crawl into their shell". This is their defence.

- *The overprotective parents.* Children who grow up with overprotective parents are more likely to become timid, since their parents' attitude diminishes the child's ability to take initiatives, to choose their friends, to explore new interests and to become socially independent.

- *Excessive criticism and rejection*, which creates a sense of worthlessness and humiliation. The child learns to accept criticism and this creates low self-esteem, i.e. poor image of his personal worth.

- *Insecure attachment with parents.* The type of relationship and the quality of a child's relationships with its parents determines the quality of its future relations with its peers and the broader environment. When these relationships are not based on the acceptance of the child's personality, on love and encouragement, the child feels insecure and becomes emotionally isolated.

Timidity and shyness become a problem when they are considered permanent traits and the child is characterised as timid. The timid child usually tends to avoid group activities such as school celebrations, performances, etc. because it will be exposed to the public eye.

The greatest risk for parents is not to treat this emotional reaction in time, because timid children usually do not disturb with their behaviour, they do not rebel, and are not disobedient; so it may go unnoticed.

WHAT SHOULD PARENTS DO?

Above all, we have to accept our child's weaknesses and shortcomings and aim at strengthening its character. We need to earnestly tell our child that we love it whatever it does and that it need not be afraid of failure. Failure, in fact, will show it the way for future success.

It is necessary to constantly encourage and praise it when it does something different and important and to emphasise its special talents that may not always be obvious, i.e. music, painting, etc. Under no circumstances should you compare it with siblings or its friends and we should, in fact, guide other family members in the same direction so that our child feels it is living in a warm, supportive family environment with security and stability.

We should encourage our child to create friendships by being social ourselves and we should let it take the initiative in matters that concern it.

We must focus on their successes rather than on their failures. In this way, we give them positive incentives to set more goals. "You had eight correct answers today; I hope tomorrow they will be 10."

Experiences and the Unconscious

In each event, there is a real dimension and a psychic one. It is true that the psychological behaviour of a person is the result of the influence of his unconscious and forgotten needs, wishes and guilt.

We all carry small or big, positive or negative experiences from the past, which, as usual, follow us throughout the course of our family life and find release and satisfaction, false of course, in the hope that they will be solved in the present via our child. In such a case, the child feels "compelled" to take care of us and often "confuses" itself with us. This experience is usually expressed through manifestations of stress, anger or emotional regression on behalf of the child.

A characteristic example is the case of a parent who experienced stress, fear and distress and internalised these feelings during their school years, but who have carried them to the present in the form of unjustifiable tension; a tension which the child perceives and experiences without being able to interpret the cause. Such a child will very often exhibit symptoms of hyperactivity and the loss of a sense of time.

Can we interpret our latent behaviour as resulting from unresolved issues of the past that influenced us negatively? If the answer is yes, then we might distance ourselves from them; we might set limits between our Self (as an internal child) and our biological needs as adults. What will we accomplish with this? We will function as consciously as possible when faced with events and situations in which our behaviour will play a decisive role in the success or failure of all we wish to apply in the upbringing and education of our children.

Through this process of catharsis and redefinition as psychological entities, we become mentally healthy persons and, as a result, we can raise mentally healthy children. We can love ourselves and show it with our actions. A child has no difficulty in believing the love and the words of his parent when he sees that his parent's life is proof of this love for oneself. How can a parent teach love, emotional give-and-take, caring and sharing, when he doesn't experience these things himself as a unique personality or even in his relationship?

There is no better example we can give our children than when we offer "care without obligations" and we lead a healthy life of self-fulfilment on all levels.

Epilogue

Now that this journey of reading has been completed, we hope to have conveyed the enthusiasm, perseverance and passion that led us to write this book. Let us not let any opportunity go to waste in the miracle of life that unfolds before us and promises us that we can enjoy happiness and become complete as parents and as people.

For, as we have already stated, we don't get a second chance to play this role again in our lives and to re-experience daily activities with our children and our family in the same way that we have been doing.

There is something more in our family life, something more in the first and important school of life. Something more for the continuation of life...

...OUR CHILDREN

Author Resumes

Anthi Sideris

Anthi Sideris was born in Evia in 1969. In 1990, she graduated from the Athens University of Economics and Business, and since 1989, she has been working in the private sector.

She is the mother of two children. She is greatly interested in education, as expressed through this collaborative project as well as through a number of training seminars she has attended, such as:

- E-seminar: "Parent Training" (November 2011) with Panagiotis Regoukos (seminar lecturer, author, speaker – he is the first trainer to introduce applied psychology in education and organisation).

- "Learning Difficulties and Inclusive Education", organised by the School of Education of the University of Nicosia in collaboration with the UNESCO Chair of the University of Nicosia (June 2014).

- "Basic principles of assertive behaviour and communication," (Anastasia Sofianopoulou, Psychologist, April 2012)

- "Life Strategy. The psychology of higher efficiency," (Akis Agelakis, Authorised Trainer, Counsellor & Life Coach, March 2013)

- "How to achieve personal and professional goals," (Akis Agelakis, Authorised Trainer, Counsellor & Life Coach, June 2010).

Anastasios Brass

Anastasios Brass has four children and four grandchildren to date. He graduated from the University of Piraeus and the Department of Social Work, and also received a post-graduate degree from the Centre for Social Studies, University of Piraeus.

- Since 1980, he has been working as a Family Counsellor.

- He was the director of the National Welfare Organisation for 15 years and then of open health care institutions.

- For 10 years, he worked as a temporary professor at the Technological Educational Institute of Athens in the Department of Social Work.

- For 21 years, he worked for two large groups of companies [ETMA SA and Kambas SA (Boutari Group)] as Head of Human Resources, as Head of Social Services and as Director of Administrative Services.

- For seven years, he worked as a general manager and as a training manager in vocational training centres.

- For four years, he was head of the department to combat exclusion of specific groups from the labour market.

- For 11 years, he collaborated with and appeared on social television programmes as a Family Counsellor.

- For 40 years, he has been a speaker at seminars for organisations, large enterprises and vocational training centres.

Other activities:

- He has written the book *Simple solutions to everyday family problems* and numerous presentations for the vocational training centres.

- He has published articles on social issues in scientific journals, in publications of the Union of Parents, the magazine *My Child and I*, and other well-known magazines as well as business journals.

- He is a regular speaker in his capacity as a family counsellor to parents of kindergarten, primary and secondary school pupils and students, and members of the Cultural Associations in Attica and in the provinces.

- He was president of the Parents' Association of primary and secondary school students for 15 years, and a member of the Parents' Board of Agia Paraskevi.

- He organises special municipal educational summer programmes for primary school children.

EFTHYMIA GLYMITSA

Effie (Efthymia) Glymitsa was born in Athens in 1976. She graduated from the Varvakeio School in 1993 and from the Faculty of Primary Education in Athens.

She worked as a teacher in the private schools 'Ionios' and 'G. Zoe'. Since 2003, she has been working in public education. In 2012, she completed a two-year postgraduate programme in Special Education at the Aegean University.

She participated as a delegate in the 3rd Congress of Special Education (11-14 April 2013) and presented her work, *The Little Prince learns to read!: Educational activities for phonological awareness for a second-year primary-school student with severe learning difficulties*, and in the National

Conference of the Scientific Association for the Promotion of Innovation in Education "Education in the ICT Era" held in Athens on 19 and 20 October 2013.

In 2013, she successfully completed the 50-hour training programme *The Family in the Modern Era.*

She has written an article entitled "Some Ideas on How to Make Children Love Books" published in the *Ekpaidevo Mikrous kai Megalous Magazine* in 2011.

Helen Tsirgioti

Helen was born in Avlonari of Evoia in 1967. She studied at the Department of Preschool Education at Aristotle University in Thessaloniki (1985-1989).

In the year 2000, she was appointed in the public sector and from 2004 until today, she has been headmistress of the all-day kindergarten in Avlonarion in Evia. She has implemented innovative programmes of the Ministry of Education (the smooth transition to primary school), health education programmes, environmental education and cultural programmes.

She has taken part in:

- many educational seminars which have been organised by various institutions and school counsellors from 2000 to date.

- the seminar "Psychosocial problems of culturally different and disadvantaged population groups." (September-December 1994).

She has published the article "*An Action Plan for Art Education in Kindergarten - Getting to Know the Work of Painters*" published in the journal *Gefyres* (issue 50, January-February 2010, Doudoumi Publications).

KATERINA ECONOMOU

Katerina Economou graduated from Regent's Col-
lege in London and acquired the specialty of psycho-
therapist in 1993. She continued her studies at the
City University of London and specialised in psychoanalytic psychotherapy through motion for children
with developmental, neurological and psycho-emo-
tional difficulties (1997). She then worked for seven
years at Queen Mary's Hospital in London with children displaying features of these disorders.

After she returned to Greece (2000) and to date, she has had a private practice and works as a psychoanalyst for children, adolescents
and adults (trained by the Hellenic Society of Psychoanalytic Psychotherapy).

Reviews - Comments from parents and educators

Basic child-rearing principles for the early years of a child in the modern social arena ... Correct behaviour and ways of handling-managing sensitive hearts and pure minds. A book that stands out for its clarity and simplicity in the way facts and events are presented. Accessible and simple, with clarity, socially comprehensible to all and for all, a "manual" with many real examples for both new and experienced parents interested in learning details of substance that will help them come closer to their child.

Authoritarianism and the rigid way of dealing with the sensitive soul of a child, which was a hindrance for generations of Greeks, is now history and belongs to the past ... The modern approach, our changing philosophy and way of thinking, the directness, simplicity and the attempt to deepen the understanding of the real needs of a child in its infancy. It is now imperative for any modern parent who wants to be close to his child, as his best friend, as the person who is really interested in deepening his soul and mind.

Congratulations to the entire writing team! You approached the subject with simplicity-seriousness, yet with the profundity and detail that unfortunately even today many parents and teachers are unaware of. It is a wonderful stimulus for all those who are really interested in learning about their child's soul. You could be a parent, you could be a godparent; you may be a relative or just an observer of a social wrongdoing. You can offer a lot, as long as you really want to ... this special "manual" will be a special asset for everyone.

Michael Delis
parent
12/16/2014

Excellent work by the whole writing team!

WE LIKED IT BECAUSE...

It is a collective project that involves issues that are important for a parent, for a teacher, but also for anyone dealing with children. The authors are from different backgrounds: Anastasios Brass, counsellor; Efthymia Glymitsa, a primary school teacher; Helen Tsirgioti, a preschool teacher; Katerina Economou, a psychoanalyst for children, adolescents and adults; and Anthi Sideris, an economist and mother, who is in charge of the project.

For this reason the knowledge provided by this book is *multifaceted* and helps the reader to become *informed* about, *understand* and then to *act* in the best possible way. It contains *information* and *advice* on the following topics:

- the family and its role in child development

- educating at home and preparing children for school

- kindergarten

- primary school

- summer holidays

- the transition from primary to secondary school

- addressing school adjustment difficulties.

The texts are written in an easily comprehensible way without tiring scientific terms and language that appeal only to a small portion of readers. That is why it can be read without confusing the reader, in the hope that it will help readers understand important issues in the development and progress of children.

A book that appeals to both parents and teachers who want something extra for the family, their children and their school.

Marlene Kefalidou
Kindergarten teacher-musician (Thessaloniki)
Chief Editor of KindyKids.gr

I read the book *Family and School*, which was really very interesting. It is a book that wins you over from the first page. It is an enlightening book, with heartfelt emotions, with a feeling that it embraces our children, our families, our lifestyles, and our personal relationships.

It is a very pleasant read, well written with nice vivid language. It is a guide that teaches the parent-reader some very important lessons in a simple and understandable way. Because I am a mother with a child in primary school and I have many concerns, this book helped me to better understand my child and his needs.

I think I was really lucky that I got my hands on this book. Every time I want to make sure I am doing the right thing for my child; I refer to it. The ideas and examples proposed for school are very easy for parents to implement.

Helen Mamali
parent

I read the book and it really reminded me of the time when I was pregnant with my daughter. I consulted books about pregnancy and infancy to learn more than I already knew or heard, and I was continuously leafing through books.

Now, after having read this book, I feel exactly the same. I have already consulted it twice. You come back to it. It provides "magical" and simple solutions that can be applied because children are simpler and purer in their relations with others. Honestly, it is very helpful, giving advice and solutions exactly where you need them.

Finally there are, in my opinion, three types of parents:

1. Those who try and then give up either because they can't take it any longer, or because they realise it wasn't what they wanted in their lives.

2. Those who, although they try in their own way, remain lukewarm, giving their children only the present.

3. Those that truly care and try to be close to their child.

This book is spiritual food for those wanting to experience the daily relationship with their child.

Xanthoula Karampigka
parent
Xanthi

REFERENCES

Greek Bibliography

Agapitos-Chalmpe, Voula (2010). *To yperkinētiko paidi kai tēn prōtē scholikē ēlikia.* [The hyperactive child in preschool and early school age]. Athens: Pedio.

Bagakis, C., Didahou, E., Valmas, F., Loumakou, M. & Pomonis, M. (2003). *Ē omalē metabasē paidiōn apo to nēpiagōgio sto dēmotiko kai ē prosarmogē toys stēn A' taxē.* [The smooth transition of children from kindergarten to primary school and their adjustment to the first year]. Athens: Metaihmio.

Bitsianis, Anthony (2011). *Scholikē mathēsē kai epitychia xōris agchos.* [School learning and success without stress]. Athens: Metaihmio.

Brass, Anastasios (1996). *Entharrynsē-Apotharrynsē-Prostateytikotēta.* [Encouragement-Discouragement-Protectiveness] (publication for the Parent-Teacher Association of the municipality of Agia Paraskevi, Attiki).

Brass, Anastasios (2008). *Aples lyseis sta kathēmerina problēmata tēs oikogeneias.* [Simple solutions to everyday family problems] (manual for trainee family counsellors for the municipalities of Attiki within the framework of the "EQUALS" programme of the EU).

Brettos, C. & Kapsalis, A. (1997). *Analytiko Programma: Schediasmos – axiologēsē – anamorphōsē.* [Analytical Curriculum: Design-evaluation-reform]. Athens: Ellinika Grammata.

Flessa, Vicky (journalist) (2011). *Synenteyxē me ton Dēmētrē Karagiannē.* [Interview with Dimitris Karagiannis]. On TV Programme *Sta Akra*

Hatzidimou, Dimitris (2007). *Eisagōgē stēn Paidagōgikē: Symbolē stē diaxysē tēs paidagōgikēs skepsēs.* [Introduction to Pedagogy: Contributing to the dissemination of pedagogical thinking]. Athens: Kyriakidis Bros SA

Kalantzi-Azizi, A. (1995). *Epharmosmenē klinikē psychologia sto chōro toy scholeioy.* [Applied clinical psychology at school]. Athens: Ellinika Grammata.

Kalantzi-Azizi, A. & Paritsi, N. (Eds.) (1990). *Oikogeneia: Psychokoinōnikes, psychotherapeytikes proseggiseis.* [Family: psychosocial, psychotherapeutic approaches]. Athens: Ellinika Grammata.

Kapatou, Alexandra (2013). *Oi goneis kanoyn tē diaphora.* [Parents make the difference]. Athens: Minos.

Kapsalis, A. (1998). *Axiologēsē kai bathmologia sto dēmotiko scholeio.* [Assessment and grading in primary school]. Athens: G. and K. Dardanos.

Karapetsas, D. B. (1993). *Ē dyslexia sto paidi Diagnōsē kai therapeia.* [Dyslexia in children: diagnosis and treatment]. Athens: Ellinika Grammata.

Koptsis, Alexander & Nakos, Alexandra. *Ē metabasē apo to Nēpaigōgeio sto Dēmotiko kai apo to Dēmotiko sto Gymnasio kai ē parallēlē proetoimasia gia tē dieykolynsē tēs.* [The transition from kindergarten to primary school and from primary to secondary school and the parallel preparation for its facilitation]. Retrieved: February 2nd, 2014 by http://stavgros.files.wordpress.com/2011/07/12-h-didaktiki-twn thetikwn-epistimwn.pdf

Krivos, Spyros (2007). *Paidagōgikē Epistēmē: Basikē Thematikē.* [Teaching Science: Basic Theme]. Athens: Gutenberg.

Kyriazis, Urania (2010). *Ē oikosystēmikē proseggisē.* [The ecosystemic approach]. *Behaviour at school: Taking advantage of opportunities, facing problems.* Koliadi, A. Emmanuel (Ed.), Athens.

Matsagouras, Elias (2008a). *Omadosynergatikē Didaskalia kai Mathēsē* [Group cooperation teaching and learning]. Athens: Grigoris.

Matsagouras, Elias (2008b). *Ē scholikē taxē: chōros, omada, peitharchia, methodos.* [The classroom: space group, discipline method]. Athens: Grigoris.

Matsagouras, Elias (2011). *Theōria kai praxē tēs didaskalias.* [Theory and practice of teaching]. Athens: Gutenberg.

Ministry of National Education and Religious Affairs. Pedagogical Institute (2000).

Dēmotiko Scholeio kai Goneis: Oikodomōntas mia dēmioyrgikē schesē. [Primary school and Parents: Building a creative relationship]. Athens: 2nd CSF.

Ministry of National Education and Religious Affairs. Ph. 50. / 92/57655 / C1 / 05.06.2007. *Innovative interventions in all-day kindergarten.*

Ministry of National Education and Religious Affairs. *Special service application CSF programmes* (2008). Parent Guide. Athens.

Panteliadou, S. (2000). *Mathēsiakes dyskolies kai ekpaideytikē praxē: Ti kai giati;* [Learning disabilities and educational practice: What and Why?] Athens: Ellinika Grammata.

Panteliadou, S. & Botsias, G. (2007). *Mathēsiakes dyskolies: Basikes ennoies kai charaktēristika.* [Learning difficulties: basic concepts and features]. Volos: Graphima.

Papadatos, John (2010). *Psychikes diataraches kai mathēsiakes dyskolies paidiōn kai ephēbōn.* [Mental disorders and learning difficulties of children and adolescents]. Athens: Gutenberg.

Paraskevopoulos, I. (1985).). *Exelektikē Psychologia, 2os Tomos: Proscholikē ēlikia.* [Developmental Psychology, 2nd Volume: Preschool]. Athens: Self-published.

Paraskevopoulos, I. (1985).). *Exelektikē Psychologia, 3os Tomos: Scholikē ēlikia* [Developmental Psychology, 3rd Volume: School age]. Athens: Self-published.

Philippidou, Kiki (2004). *Ēsaia xoreye kai ystera...ti;* [Isaiah was dancing and then ... what?]. Athens: Empeiria Ekdotiki.

Pinteris, George (2005). *Syntrophikotēta kai aytonomia stis scheseis toy zeygarioy.* [Companionship and autonomy in couple relationships]. Athens: Papasotiriou.

Porpodas, R. D. (1988). *Dyslexia: Ē eidikē diatarachē stē mathēsē toy graptoy logoy.* [Dyslexia: The specific disorder in learning the written language]. Self-publication.

Porpodas, R. D. (1996).). *Gnōstikē psychologia: Ē diadikasia tēs mathēsēs.* [Cognitive psychology: The process of learning]. Volume One. Athens: Self-published.

Porpodas, K. D. (2003). *Ē mathēsē kai oi dyskolies tēs (Gnōstikē proseggisē).* [Learning and its difficulties (cognitive approach)]. Patras: Self-published.

Psara, Georgia (2008). *Problēmata symperiphoras sto scholeio me tēn oikosystēmikē proseggisē, Themata diacheirisēs problēmatōn scholikēs taxes.* [Behavioural problems at school with the ecosystemic approach, Themes classroom management problems], Volumes A and B. Makri-Botsari, Evanthia (Ed.) Athens: Ministry of Education and Religious Affairs and Pedagogical Institute.

Sakkas, B. (2002). *Mathēsiakes dyskolies kai oikogeneia* .[Learning disabilities and the family]. Athens: Atrapos.

Sotiriou, A. & Zafiropoulou, M. (2003). *Allages stēn ennoia toy eaytoy tōn paidiōn kata tē metabasē toys apo to nēpiagōgeio sto dēmotiko scholeio*. [Changes in the sense of self of children in their transition from kindergarten to primary school]. *Psychology* 10 (1), 96 118 (http://mzafiroplab.ece.uth.gr/27.pdf).

Spantidakis, I. (2004). *Problēmata paragōgēs graptoy logoy paidiōn scholikēs ēlikias*. [Problems producing written language in schoolchildren]. Athens: Ellinika Grammata.

Theodosakis, Dimitris (2011). *Ē synaisthēmatikē noēmosynē sto sygchrono scholeio*. [Emotional intelligence in the modern school]. Athens: Grigoris.

Travlos, Anthony (1998). *Psychokiētikē anaptyxē* [Psychomotor development]. Athens: Savalas.

Triantafyllidi, Erato (2010). *Egcheiridio Ey Zēn: Odēgos zōēs apo toys archaioys Ellēnes sophoys*. [Well-being Manual: Life Guide from ancient Greek sages]. Athens: Archetypo.

Trilianos, Thanassis (2009). *Ē Parōthēsē toy mathētē gia mathēsē*. [Motivating students to learn]. Athens: Self-published.

Tzouriadou, M. (1995). *Paidia mē eidikes ekpaideytikes anagkes: Mia psychopaidagōgikē proseggisē*. [Children with special educational needs: a psycho-educational approach]. Thessaloniki: Prometheus.

Tzouriadou M. (2008). *Mathēsiakes dyskolies* on the programme *Analytika Programmata Mathēsiakōn Dyskoliōn – Enēmerōsē – Eyaisthētopoiēsē*. [Detailed Programmes for Learning Disabilities - Information – Awareness]. Downloaded on February 25th 2014 from http://hdl.handle.net/10795/957

Vosniadou, Stella (2001). *Eisagōgē stēn psychologia*. [Introduction to psychology]. Athens: Gutenberg.

Vrynioti, K. (2007). *Scholikē entaxē kai oikogeneia: Mia ereynētikē proseggisē tōn empeiriōn tōn paidiōn stēn aphetēria tēs scholikēs zōēs apo tēn skopia tōn goneōn*. [School Integration and Family: A research approach of children's experiences in starting school life from the perspective of parents]. *Education sciences* 2, 67-87.

Vrynioti K. & Matsagouras, I. (2005). *H metabasē apo to nēpiagōgeio sto dēmotiko scholeio: Mia oikosystēmikē ereynētikē proseggisē tōn koinōnikōn sxeseōn tōn archaiōn mathētōn kai mathētriōn stē scholikē taxē.* [The transition from kindergarten to primary school: An ecosystemic research approach of the social relations of beginner pupils in the classroom]. *Pedagogical Review* 40, 78-102.

Xochellis, Panagiotis (2005). *Eisagōgē stēn Paidagōgikē: Themeliōdē problēmata tēs Paidagōgikēs Epistēmēs.* [Introduction to Pedagogy: Fundamental problems of Pedagogical Science]. Athens: Kyriakidis Bros SA

Zafiropoulou, M. & Kalantzi-Azizi, A. (2011). *Prosarmogē sto scholeio: Prolēpsē kai antimetōpisē dyskoliōn.* [Adjustment at school: Prevention and treatment difficulties]. Athens: Pedio.

FOREIGN BIBLIOGRAPHY

Alberti, Robert E.& Emmons, Michael L. (2008). *Your Perfect Right: Assertiveness and Equality in Your Life and Relationships.* Athens: Patakis.

American Psychiatric Association (1994). *Diagnostic and Statistical Manual of Mental Disorders, 4th ed. (DSM-IV).* Washington, DC.

Berger, Maurice & Gravillon, Isabelle (2004). *Mes Parents Se Separent,* Athens: State.

Bloom, Benjamin (1985). *Developing Talent in Young People.*

Blumenthal, Erik (1998). *Love and Marriage.* Athens: Filistor.

Buscaglia, Leo (1988). *Living, Loving and Learning.* Athens: Glaros.

Dattilio, F.M. and Padesky, C.A. (1995). *Couple Therapy: Cognitive-Behavioural Approach.* Translation: N. Charila; editor: A. Kalantzi-Azizi. Athens: Ellinika Grammata.

Dinkmeyer, Don; McKay, Gary D. (2007). *Parenting Teenagers: Systematic Training for Effective Parenting of Teens.* Athens: Thymari.

Fulghum, Robert (1988). *All I Really Need to Know I Learned in Kindergarten.* Athens: Lychnos.

Gardner, Howard (1983). *Frames of Mind.* New York: Basic Books

Goleman, D. (1998). *Working with Emotional Intelligence.* London: Bloomsbury Publishing.

Gottman, John (2011). *The Heart of Parenting*. Athens: Pedio

Harris, A.J., & Sipay, E.R. (1980). *How to Increase Reading Ability: A Guide to Developmental and Remedial Methods*. New York: Longman.

Lazarus, Arnold A. and Lazarus Clifford N. (2003).*The 60-second shrink*. Athens: Esoptron.

Littauer, Florence (1999). *Personality Plus*. Athens: Kleidarithmos.

Mathelin, Catherine and Costa-Prades, Roland (2005). *Comment survivre en famille*. Athens: Christos Dardanos.

McDowell, Josh and Day, Dick (2004). *How To Be A Hero To Your Kids*. Athens: Logos.

Miller, Bonnie (2003). *Communicating with Children*. Athens: Greek Institute of Study and Research of Difficulties of Learning.

Moore-Mallinos, Jennifer (2006a). *Do You Have a Secret? (Let's Talk About It!)* Athens: Sabbalas.

Moore-Mallinos, Jennifer (2006b). *I Remember (Let's Talk About It!)* Athens: Sabbalas.

Moore-Mallinos, Jennifer (2006c). *The Colours of the Rainbow (Let's Talk About It!)* Athens: Sabbalas.

Moore-Mallinos, Jennifer (2006d). *When My Parents Forgot How to Be Friends (Let's Talk About It!)* Athens: Sabbalas.

Nathan, Robert, and Linda Hill. *Career Counselling*. Athens: Metaixmio.

Papazian, Sandy (2002). *Growing Up with Joey* (Review by: Dr Jack Wetter).

Porpora, Tracey, Guest Author. *5 Ways to Spark your Children's Enthusiasm for Summer Reading*. Downloaded on 20 January 2014 from www.about.com

Steinberg, Laurence (2006). *The Ten Basic Principles of Good Parenting*. Athens: Dioptra.

Taylor, Betsy (2003). *What Kids Really Want That Money Can't Buy*. Athens: Fytrakis.

www.ingramcontent.com/pod-product-compliance
Lightning Source LLC
Chambersburg PA
CBHW081641040426

42449CB00015B/3406